THE ATTACK ON THE CANON OF SCRIPTURE

A Polemic Against Modern Gnostics

H. D. Williams, M.D., Ph.D.

THE OLD PATHS PUBLICATIONS
CLEVELAND, GEORGIA 30528

BIBLE FOR TODAY NUMBER #3345

Disclaimer

The author of this work has quoted the writers of many articles and books. This does not mean that the author endorses or recommends the works of others. If the author quotes someone, it does not mean that he agrees with all of the author's tenets, statements, concepts, or words, whether in the work quoted or any other work of the author. There has been no attempt to alter the meaning of the quotes; and therefore, some of the quotes are long in order to give the entire sense of the passage.

Copyright © 2008 by H. D. Williams
All Rights Reserved
Printed in the United States of America

Library of Congress Control Number: 2007943203
REL067030: Religion: Christian Theology - Apologetics

ISBN 978-0-9801689-2-1

All Scripture quotes are from the King James Bible except those verses compared and then the source is identified.

No part of this work may be reproduced without the expressed consent of the publisher, except for brief quotes, whether by electronic, photocopying, recording, or information storage and retrieval systems.

Address All Inquiries To:
THE OLD PATHS PUBLICATIONS, INC.
142 Gold Flume Way
Cleveland, Georgia, U.S.A.

Web: www.theoldpathspublications.com
E-mail: TOP@theoldpathspublications.com

BIBLE FOR TODAY NUMBER #3345
Web: www.biblefortoday.org
E-mail: bft@biblefortoday.org

1.0

DEDICATION

    This work is dedicated to my son, David, who has added untold joy in my life.

H. D. Williams, M.D., Ph.D.

CONTENTS

TITLE	PAGE
DEDICATION..	3
CONTENTS...	5
ABBREVIATIONS...	9
DEFINITIONS...	11
PREFACE...	17
Scripture or Theories?..	17
Which Word is Correct: Debate or Attack?.............	18
Gnostics Are Always Involved.................................	20
Modern and Postmodern Gnosticism......................	21
History Must be Used With Care............................	22
The Scarlet Thread in the COS................................	23
There is a Mystery..	24
Confusion Instigated by Suppositions.....................	26
Suppositions..	28
Scholars and Philosophy...	28
The New Academic Course: "Canon Criticism"......	30
The Shift in the Attack by Canon Criticism............	31
CHAPTER 1: WHAT IS THE CANON OF SCRIPTURE?	33
The KJB is The Canon Preserved in English............	34
The COS is Mentioned in Scripture	35
The Mistake of Naturalistic Textual Critics.............	36
The Attack on the COS Uncovered..........................	40
Conservative Researcher's Evidence.......................	41
CHAPTER 2: SCHOLAROLATRY............................	45
Scholars Using Scholarolatry..................................	45
Protecting Our Children From "Scholarolatry".......	47
CHAPTER 3: GOD'S YOUNG MESSENGER WARNS "SCHOLARS"	49
The Inspiration of the Almighty..............................	50
Scholars Are Like The Ostrich.................................	52
What Have The Scholars Done?..............................	54

CHAPTER 4: THE ASSAULT ON THE OLD TESTAMENT CANON 57
Attacks Thwarted by Copies of All His Words 58
The Attack on the Canon by Indifference, Neglect, and Apostasy 60
The Attack on the Canon Answered by Wrath, Sometimes Delayed 61
Remember: 1. The Canon of the Old Testament is Preserved .. 62
Remember: 2. God's Warning 63
Remember: 3. There Are False Claims 63

CHAPTER 5: THE ATTACK ON THE NT CANON 65
Many Corrupt the Words of God 65
The Septuagint (LXX) 65
Other Attacks Through the Centuries 67
Canon Criticism 69
Scholars Claim Fraudulent Books Are in the Sacred Canon 71
More False Claims 72
Claims of False Books 74
False Claims Refuted 75

CHAPTER 6: WHO WERE THE GNOSTICS? 79
1. Gnostics Often "Went Out From" Bible Believing Churches   80
2. Gnostics and Scholars Are Similar 85
3. Gnostic Beliefs 87
4. Attractions to Gnosticism 88
5. Tendencies of Gnosticism 88
6. Gnostics and Scholars Compared 89
7. The Apostate School With a Significant Influence 90
8. Examples of Modern Gnostics 94
9. Where Did Gnosticism Start? 95
10. The Gnostic Marcion 96
11. Other Gnostics 98
12. Historical Information Thwarts Attempt to Undermine Scripture 98

CHAPTER 7: A CANON WITHIN A CANON? 101
Be No More Children Tossed To and Fro 102

CHAPTER 8: THE GAME SCHOLARS PLAY 105
A Spoof 105
Redefining Words 106

Inserts?.. 107
Q Document?... 108

CHAPTER 9: SCHOLARS WANT TO CHANGE THE BIBLE.. 111
Add to or Reduce the Canon?.................................... 111
Will This Achieve Unity?.. 112
Tolerance?.. 112

CHAPTER 10: AN ALLEGORY.. 115

CHAPTER 11: CONCLUSION... 121
The Curse.. 121
Warnings... 123
The Answer.. 125
Remember His Words... 125

APPENDICES... 131
APPENDIX 1: Robert Dick Wilson............................... 131
APPENDIX 2: Cross Reference Table: Early Writings That Confirm the Early COS.. 134
APPENDIX 3: Quotes of Canon by Ignatius in His Letters to Various Persons and Churches.................................. 138
APPENDIX 4: Surviving a College Education.............. 143
APPENDIX 5: Relevant Quotes................................... 144
APPENDIX 6: The Formation of The New Testament Canon.. 150
APPENDIX 7: Crime Graphs....................................... 152
APPENDIX 8: Crime Stats.. 156
APPENDIX 9: Approximate Speculative Terms Used in *Lost Christianities* Compared to *Revision Revised*............ 158
APPENDIX 10: Exercise Care Reading the Following Books... 159

BIBLIOGRAPHY.. 161
INDEX.. 165
ABOUT THE AUTHOR... 169

ABBREVIATIONS

AFTs = accurate and faithful translations
ca. = circa = approximately
cf = compare
COS = Canon of Scripture
CT = critical text
DBS = Dean Burgon Society
DSS = Dead Sea Scrolls
e.g. = for example
ERV = English Revised Version
ff = and following
i.e. = that is
KJB = King James Bible
LXX = seventy; it is frequently used for the Septuagint
MS = manuscript
MSS = manuscripts
NASV = New American Standard Version
NIV = New International Version
NLB = New Living Bible
NT = New Testament
OT = Old Testament
RSV = Revised Standard Version
RT = Received Text
TaNaK = Torah, Nebiim, and Ketubim
TT = Traditional Text
W/H = Westcott and Hort

DEFINITIONS

Alexandrian: a term often applied to works that are believed to be from Alexandria, Egypt and the immediate surrounding area. The best evidence available demonstrates that the manuscripts originating in Alexandria were corrupted by the many cults that were based there. A scholar is sometimes called an Alexandrian because he favors manuscripts from Alexandra.

Apocrypha: books that are not recognized as inspired written during the intertestamental period and early post-Apostolic era. They are included in the Septuagint and Latin Vulgate versions of the Bible. Origen included them in his Septuagint version called the LXX as historically important. The Roman Catholics include them as part of the Canon of Scripture. They are not included in the Protestant or Baptist Bibles, although they were placed in the early King James Bible for historical reasons. Many of the books were written by individuals with pseudonyms and are called the pseudepigrapha, which means false letters or books.

Apograph: copies of original manuscripts. They are often the result of many copies repeatedly made through the centuries. The TT/RT apographs are virtually identical.

Autograph: the original manuscripts upon which the Apostles and prophets recorded the inspired Words received from God. They are no longer extant.

Canon of Scripture: the definitions are all over the place. However, the correct definition is the sixty-six books of the Bible recognized as the inspired Words of God by the institutions given the responsibility to preserve them. These institutions are the Jewish nation Israel and the Bible-believing New Testament churches. A recorded list does not establish the Canon of Scripture. Through the centuries, The priesthood of believers influenced by the Holy Spirit guarded and protected the Words of God that were recorded by the prophets and Apostles. No council, government, committee, or other organization was given the responsibility by God. The OT Canon was closed during Ezra's time. The New Testament Canon was closed after the Apostle John recorded the book of Revelation.

Canon: rule (ruler), a measure, standard

Canonical: a book recognized as a part of the Canon of Scripture. The names of the books vary from denomination to denomination. The Jewish Canon has been settled since the time of Ezra. The Roman Catholics added the apocrypha to their canon in the mid-sixteenth century.

Charismatic (Movement): is an interfaith movement emphasizing religious experiences such as the second "baptism in the Holy Spirit," accompanied by "speaking in tongues" and miraculous "sign" gifts at the expense of biblical authority and sound biblical interpretation. The movement encourages ecumenism. The movement varies from church to church and denomination to denomination.

Codex: manuscripts of papyrus or animal hide bound together like a book.

Community: a term that postmodernists have personalized in place of "church" (e.g. "our community," "community of faith," or "intergenerational community").

COS: see Canon of Scripture.

Critical text: a text formed by scholars that is constructed from a very few corrupted manuscripts which originated in the city of Alexandria known for its cults. The CT is often called the Alexandrian Text.

Dialectical materialism: the belief that reality stops with the material universe and the tension created by attempts to control it or have authority over it. History revolves around the class struggles over materialism.

Gnosticism: the belief that knowledge leads to salvation through the ability to understand esoteric, mystical, or transcendental things about the universe.

Hermeneutics: for all practical purposes is interpretation of a Biblical passage.

Inscripturated Words: The Words recorded by God's Apostles and prophets in the sixty-six books of the Bible. Not all of the Words spoken by God from heaven or by the Lord Jesus Christ during the first advent are recorded in the Bible. Only the Words that God wanted us to have are inscripturated and preserved. For example, it is very likely that a letter (epistle) to the Corinthian Church was lost (1 Cor. 5:9). Perhaps a letter to the Laodiceans was also lost (Col. 4:16).

Inspiration: theologically: Dr. Thomas Strouse gives a definition, which is concise:
> "Inspiration is the process whereby the Holy Spirit led the writers of scripture to record accurately His very words; the product of this process was the inspired original."[1]

Knowledge: general awareness or possession of information, facts, ideas, truth, or principles. Recent postmodern philosophers, such as Michael Foucault, insist that:
> "knowledge makes power" is not monodirectional, but rather, "power also produces knowledge."[2]

Therefore, Bart Ehrman, a postmodernist, claims Gnostic books that should have been in the Scripture are not included because the "orthodox" early Christians were in power.

Majority Text: This term formally meant the text used by the majority of sanctified churches called the Traditional/Received Text. However, the term has been hijacked by some textual critics and applied to a text dependent upon examination of **all** the ancient manuscripts. However, this is an impossible task secondary to the poor quality of the texts, access to them, finances, and certainty that all texts are available. Usually, the term is applied to a text based upon the work of Von Soden. His work is often criticized for its inadequacy.

Mysticism:
> "belief in intuitive spiritual revelation; in religion the belief that personal communication or union with the divine is achieved through intuition, faith, ecstasy, or sudden insight rather than through rational thought (Encarta)."

Neo-Evangelicalism:
> "is the philosophical movement which subjects cooperation in ministry to social and spiritual need rather than biblical authority. It endeavors to infiltrate society with a

---

[1] Dr. Thomas Strouse, Dean, Emmanuel Baptist Theological Seminary, "The Translation Model Predicted by Scripture" (http://www.emmanuel-newington.org/seminary/resources/KJV_Model.pdf).
[2] Millard J Erickson, *The Postmodern World, Discerning the Times and the Spirit of Our Age* (Crossway Books, Wheaton, IL, 2002) p. 41.

respectable gospel through emphasizing toleration and theological pragmatism. It seeks to present a united voice in evangelicalism by bringing together theological liberals and conservative evangelicals in cooperative efforts and movements."[3]

Neo-Orthodoxy:
"is the movement which, while affirming the transcendence of God, the finiteness and sinfulness of man, and the necessity of supernatural divine revelation of truth; seriously departs from orthodoxy, redefines biblical terminology, accepts the views of destructive higher criticism, denies the inerrancy of the Scriptures as historic revelation, accepts religious experience as the criterion of truth, and abandons other important truths of the Christian faith."[4]

Parousia: usually refers to the second coming of the Lord Jesus Christ, but it has taken on the meaning of any of God's visits to earth. It simply means "coming" or "presence" according to *Strong's Greek Dictionary*.

Plenary: all the words in a text; full, unlimited; no words excluded.

Postmodernism: although there are many variations and significant overlapping, three basic views are noted. (1) Postmodernism is (a) an attitude of uncertainty about most things and (b) applicable truth is derived from a person's community (subjectivism), (2) Postmodernism is extreme selfism (subjectivism) and uncertainty about everything. Although there may be absolute truth, man cannot know it. (3) Postmodernism is the belief that there is no absolute truth. Subsequently, metanarratives are rejected (i.e. God, Bible, ideas, materialism, etc.). Only the individual can determine truth for himself from his experiences of reality. All three positions are humanistic and result in rejection of absolute truth, particularly the Bible.

Proto-orthodox: literally means first in time with traditional beliefs. Scholars are giving the term a twist. They imply the first orthodox Christians achieved their authority by power. Subsequently, other legitimate beliefs were suppressed.

---

[3] www.svchapel.org/Assets/Docs/DoctrinalStatement.pdf.
[4] www.svchapel.org/Assets/Docs/DoctrinalStatement.pdf.

Definitions

Received Text (RT): the Greek manuscripts which were copies of the autographs known as apographs. The RT is the text copied and passed from sanctified church to sanctified church over the centuries. It became the text of the Reformation. The saints of the Reformation rejected the Latin Vulgate and the minority corrupted Greek texts.

Scholarolatry: the worship of scholars. This is similar to Mariolatry.

Traditional Text (TT): This text is the Received Text and a few other places (190) that were found by the KJB translators who were without equal as students of the Scriptures. They recovered the precise perfect Words lost over the centuries from the virtually identical RT. The Words were confirmed in lectionaries, church elder writings, and ancient translations or versions of the preserved apographs of the autographs. This was God's method to preserve the Words. The Words confirmed by the method of preservation chosen by God, are the exact Words of the original God-breathed Words recorded by the prophets and Apostles.

TaNaK: the tripartite OT canon, which is the writings of Moses, the prophets, and the writings. It is called the TaNaK, which is an anachronism for the Torah, Nebiim, and Ketubim.

Transcendentalism: "philosophy emphasizing reasoning **or** the divine" In regard to reasoning: a philosophical "system of philosophy, especially that of Kant, that regards the processes of reasoning as the key to knowledge of reality;" **or** in regard to the divine, a philosophical
    "system of philosophy, especially that associated with
    Ralph Waldo Emerson and other New England writers,
    that emphasizes intuition or the divine" (Encarta).
The divine is mystical, not a person, the Lord Jesus Christ, as revealed in a Holy Bible.

PREFACE

*"Howbeit when he, the Spirit of truth, is come, he will **guide you into all truth**: for he shall not speak of himself; but whatsoever he shall hear, that shall he speak: and he will shew you things to come" (John 16:13).*

*"And **that from a child thou hast known the holy scriptures**, which are able to make thee wise unto salvation through faith which is in Christ Jesus" (2 Timothy 3:15)*

*"Being born again, not of corruptible seed, but of incorruptible, by the word of God, which liveth and abideth for ever. For all flesh is as grass, and all the glory of man as the flower of grass. The grass withereth, and the flower thereof falleth away: But **the word of the Lord endureth for ever. And this is the word which by the gospel is preached unto you**" (1 Peter 1:23-25).*

This work is about the attack on the "Canon of Scripture" (COS). Many related topics will *not* be discussed. Hundreds of pages would be necessary to enumerate and explain the entire array of the attacks on the COS. This work will primarily focus upon several false theories related to the following questions. First, how were books selected for inclusion in the Bible? Second, how were books excluded? Third, how important was a list of the COS to the early sanctified churches and how necessary is a list to this generation of believers?

Scripture or Theories?

A careful exegesis and interpretation of the verses quoted above answer the questions posed. However, many scholars start with their theories rather than with Scripture. There is a shying away from the precise, pure, perfect deposit of the Words by God for man on earth. This author cannot overlook this serious penchant of present-day scholars. There is a need to answer their folly from Scripture and to respond to their suppositions about the COS.

If someone is fortunate enough to live as long as this author has, he will discover there is only one Truth on the face of this earth that is absolute and reliable. There is only one Truth that has not changed and that is verified repeatedly by history, archaeology, and providence (Mat. 24:35, Jn. 17:17, Heb. 13:8). Theories about the COS must be cast aside for what they simply are; suppositions. Personal experience and emotions must not be relied upon for determining truth. They are a trap. Only faith in the Lord Jesus Christ and His Words will lead to Truth and ultimate triumph.

Scholars' recent conjectures about the formation of the COS have launched another serious attack on the precious Words of truth. The confidence of many individuals has been disturbed by speculations about the Words given by God for man's guidance in the COS. Furthermore, many scholars in institutions of higher learning are indoctrinating our children with their speculations, which they unabashedly too often call truth. The end result is confusion for many people, especially our children, who were taught the COS is God's preserved Words to mankind. We must be ready to give them and others, who are being influenced by the very inappropriate dogmatism of scholars, answers (1 Pe. 3:15).

Which Word is Correct: Debate or Attack?

Intellectuals disguise the attack on the COS by using the term "debate." Scholars use the term to give legitimacy to what is really an all out assault on the COS. It is not even a dialectical debate to arrive at a modicum of truth. It is a war against the preserved Words in the COS.

The assailing of the books of the Bible is the foremost topic of discussion in this work. The truth pertaining to the formation of the Judaic COS and the recognition of OT and NT biblical books by apostolic, Bible-believing, sanctified churches will be addressed.

Whatever someone calls these "questions," "debates," or "arguments" instigated by academics, they are creating widespread doubt and confusion and are encouraging the departure from the Christian faith by our innocent and easily influenced children.

It is necessary to name some of the men who are putting forth their theories as truth in order to be factual. They seem far removed from the guidance of the Spirit of God; they lack clear understanding of the providential care of God. They cannot seem to grasp the consistent steadfast stand of sanctified men and sanctified churches throughout history that have protected God's Words as commanded.[5] Therefore, in the preface of this presentation, it behooves us to make a few comments pertaining to the early recognition of the COS in defense of God's Words.

It bears repeating that the present-day attack centers upon the books included and excluded from the COS. In previous centuries, honest godly men on occasion legitimately questioned a book in the COS, but not for long. For example, Luther seriously questioned the book of James. At first, he could not resolve what appeared to him to be a conflict between the book of Romans and the book of James. However, he eventually resolved the question and believed the book should be in the COS.

Sacred Wisdom surrounds the formation of the COS. Its development was not a mystical selection or an authoritarian

---

[5] H. D. Williams, M.D., Ph.D., *The Pure Words of God, Where to Find God's Words Which We Are Commanded to Receive and Keep* (The Old Paths Publications, Cleveland, GA, 2008) Chapter 2.

determination by men in seats of authority. The Wisdom comes from the Words left for us by the Trinity.

Even though there are available "lists," "authoritative councils," and early church pastors' writings that affirm the COS, the recognition of the COS comes from the knowledge of a Holy God and his declarations (Pro. 9:10). The presence of a "list" did not verify the COS nor did the date of a complete list of recognized books settle the question. As we shall see, the process of inspiration and the guidance of the Holy Spirit established the Canon. Nevertheless, the attack that rages today on the COS mirrors previous attacks over the centuries on:

1. the inspired, inerrant, infallible, precise, perfect, pure Words of God from the beginning (Gen. 3:1-2),
2. the inspiration of the Words,
3. the recording of the Words,
4. the preservation of the Words,
5. the inerrancy of the Words,
6. the infallibility of the Words, and
7. the Words overriding tradition.

Gnostics Are Always Involved.

Many cults existed in the early post-apostolic period that corrupted the Words of God. Heretical and apostate men formed cults. They were called by various names, but in general, most of them fall under the designation Gnostic and their philosophy was known as Gnosticism. The Gnostics used their penknives on Words in the books or epistles recorded by God's Apostles and prophets to remove hindrances to their speculative philosophy. Their philosophy was an amalgamation of various religions, particularly scholasticism which is Greek philosophy and Judaism mixed together. Each cult declared their 'new' work, resulting from their attack on the inscripturated Words with penknives or scissors, was the correct version of the Bible. The Apostle Paul spoke about these attacks. He said:

> *"For we are not as many, which corrupt the word of God: but as of sincerity, but as of God, in the sight of God speak we in Christ." 2 Corinthians 2:17*

Without a doubt, Paul's letters were inspired Words received from the Holy Spirit (1 Cor. 2:13). Peter mentions Paul's books were inspired Scripture (2 Pe. 3:16). The proofs of inspiration cannot be addressed in this work. The important point is that Paul also mentions the early attack on the epistles, letters, or books of the COS. Books or epistles (letters) were being fraudulently presented as his Words that he received from the Holy Spirit. He said:

> *"That ye be not soon shaken in mind, or be troubled, neither by spirit, nor by word, nor by letter **as from us**, as that the day of Christ is at hand." 2 Thessalonians 2:2*

Modern and Postmodern Gnosticism

So, even though there is a renewed postmodern attack, which is an extension of the modern attack, it is not new. Nothing under the sun is new. Modern and postmodern Gnosticism is not new. Paul's writings and other New Testament books warn about scholars, false apostles, hypocritical preachers, and unfounded theories. Today, the warnings are completely ignored (cf. 1 Cor. 1:19-20, Col. 2:8, 1 Tim. 1:3-4). For example, Paul said:

> *"But the natural man receiveth not the things of the Spirit of God: for they are foolishness unto him: neither can he*

> *know them, because they are spiritually discerned."* 1 Corinthians 2:14

The presentations in this work will not be received well by those who do not have the Spirit, by those who quench and grieve Him, by prideful men in high places, and by men protecting their income. Many men taking the position offered in this work are relieved of their jobs because of their convictions. This is similar to the firings over a stand for creationism. They may secretly understand the Truth, but they have families and responsibilities and they are prevented from taking an overt position. This author is not defending them for not speaking out, but merely presenting the facts. The influence and guidance of the Holy Spirit is quenched in light of these issues.

Many others cannot understand the literal statements in Scripture about the process of the formation of the Scriptures and their inclusion in the Bible. This does not mean anyone understands perfectly the process any more than anyone completely understands how God does miracles. A person would have to be God. We simply must accept the Truth, just as we accept the virgin birth, the resurrection, creation and many other revealed truths. We must not bring our ideas, concepts, or thoughts to Scripture. We must let Scripture speak to us. This is called *inductive* hermeneutics. Start with the jots and tittles and develop doctrine. Do not start with a personal belief or doctrine and then find Scripture to support your position or theory. This is *deductive* logic and leads to many incorrect and foolish doctrines and concepts.

History Must be Used With Care

Furthermore, history is often rewritten. It cannot be relied upon to uncover "truth." History can only be used to confirm Truth. Too many people turn to history first, then try to make the Bible fit their concept of the preservation of Scripture. This is how the attack on the COS by scholars, who propose "proto-Christians" and "proto-orthodox" theories, started. They used history to support their theories by using *deductive* logic.

History cannot be relied upon to establish Truth with certainty. However, the evidence supporting the COS found in the history of the Hebrew Masoretic Text and the TT/RT far exceeds the paltry evidence presented in favor of the constructed false Critical Text by men. The Traditional Text of the Bible is not a rewritten work. It was received.

Satan is the author of confusion. The many COS lists over the centuries exhibit the confusion of the enemy. Furthermore, the lists were created a significant number of years after the last book of the Bible was written. Also, many of the lists are substantially different. For example, when Jerome wrote the *Latin Vulgate*, he included the apocrypha for historical interest. Later, at the Roman Catholic Church's Council of Trent (1545-1563), the apocrypha was *declared* part of the COS for that denomination. The COS for the Baptist Bible and Protestant Bible does not include the apocrypha and if a publication by Baptist and Protestants happens to include it, it is only for historical interest. Some early lists include other spurious books as part of the COS. So, how did we arrive at the sixty-six books in the COS? That question will be answered later on in this work. How did the OT and NT books come to be included in the same list of Canonical books?

The Scarlet Thread in the COS

Most scholars do not understand the formation of the OT and the NT COS as separate entities that were subsequently bound together. The primary reason for this union of OT and NT books is because our Lord made it clear that the OT was about Him (cf. Lk. 24:25-27). Nevertheless, the entire process raises questions for many "scholars." They seem unable to comprehend the unifying *"scarlet thread"* that runs throughout the sixty-six books. The *"scarlet thread"* is a metaphor for the typological blood that was shed by the Old Testament sacrifices and extends into the NT until the final *"once for all"* shedding of blood by the Lord Jesus Christ. Jesus explained the connection to the couple on the road to Emmaus. *"[B]eginning at Moses and all the prophets, he expounded unto them in all the scriptures the things concerning himself"* [Lk 24:27]. The blood He shed is the "scarlet thread" that runs throughout the sixty-six books. The unity of the OT and NT is miraculous. It could come about only by the hand of an intelligence that far exceeds any human intelligence.

There is a Mystery

There is a mystery (not mystical) related to the COS, that this author believes is 'part and parcel' related to the same 'mystery' of inspiration. The mystery is related to the work of the Holy Spirit. But it is far deeper than that aspect alone. The three persons of the Godhead were completely unified in the Words given to the Apostles and prophets to be recorded. Their work from a humanistic standpoint is totally incomprehensible. It is just as incomprehensible as the involvement of the Trinity in creation. Furthermore, how did God accomplish the acts of creation? Certainly, the Holy Spirit was present from creation when *"the Spirit of God moved upon the face of the waters"* (Gen. 1:2). We have no idea how He created material "things" ex nihilo (Latin for "from nothing")! He is responsible for the *"new man"* or *"new creature"* when man is born-again. How does He do it? Those who have experienced being *"born again"* have no idea how the Spirit does it, but they know when it occurs. Lastly, speaking as a physician, when man can explain the most complex and intricate computer ever envisioned inside the microscopic nucleus of the *living* cell, then considerations for scholars pronouncements about the COS will be considered. Of course, none of these things will ever be completely understood on this side of heaven. God has restricted our knowledge so that we must live by faith in Him and His Words.

Furthermore, we have no idea what the mechanism is or how the Spirit spoke through *"holy men,"* but we know it occurred because the Scripture tells us it did. *"[H]oly men of God spake as they were moved by the Holy Ghost."* (2 Pe. 1:21). Similarly, the Holy Spirit has guided Bible-believers into the proper COS. The Scripture plainly says,

> *"Howbeit when he, the Spirit of truth, is come, he will guide you into all truth: for he shall not speak of himself; but whatsoever he shall hear, that shall he speak: and he will shew you things to come" [John 16:13, cf.1 Cor. 13:10, 2 Tim. 3:16-17).*

This verse had immediate application to the Apostles and prophets who recorded the Words of Scripture, but it also has extended application to the Spirit's guidance of the priesthood of believers into Truth through the centuries. This includes the COS.

Confusion Instigated by Suppositions

Many scholars through the years have claimed various authoritative entities determined the COS. For example, they have widely publicized the synod of Jamnia (Yavneh) in 90 A.D. as the time for the final establishment of the tripartite OT canon, which is the writings of Moses, the prophets, and the writings. It is called the TaNaK, which is an anachronism for the Torah, Nebiim, and Ketubim.

However, some scholars retracted their declarations for the purpose of the synod of Jamnia in a recent book, *The Canon Debate*. Consider the following statement.

> "Albert Sundberg recognizes that the "Council of Jamnia" hypothesis is dead."[6]

In the same book, other authors of the book demonstrate more confusion. One author declares,

> "Thus, Jesus' comment "from the blood of Abel to the blood of Zechariah" is **PROBABLY** meant to sum up Israel's history, not Israel's sacred scripture."[7]

Probably? Isn't Israel's history recorded in the "sacred scripture," which is found in certain books included in the Jews COS from Abel (in Genesis) to Zechariah (in Chronicles)? The last book in the way the Jews organize the thirty-seven books of the OT is Chronicles. Their sacred OT books are the same sacred OT books included in the NT era COS, but they are arranged in a different order.

---

[6] Lewis, Jack P.; *The Canon Debate,* Lee M. McDonald and James A. Sanders, Editors, Hendrickson Publishers, Peabody, MA, 2002, p. 162.
[7] Ibid. p. 190. (*The Canon Debate,* Chapter by Craig A. Evans).

And still another author in the *Canon Debate* in a different work, *Introduction To Biblical Interpretation*, proclaims,

> "This more liberal view may agree that it is logical to follow Jesus' lead in treating as Scripture what he, with Jews of his day, accepted as Scripture. **BUT** they insist that we simply cannot know which books he would have had embraced."[8]

These quotes demonstrate the confusion in the "scholars" camp concerning the COS. Well, some of us insist that the nation of Israel and the early church knew precisely which books were inspired. Jesus clearly stated,

> *"And he said unto them, These are the words which I spake unto you, while I was yet with you, that all things must be fulfilled, which were written in the law of Moses, and in the prophets, and in the psalms, concerning me." [Luke 24:44]* and, *"That upon you may come all the righteous blood shed upon the earth, from the blood of righteous Abel unto the blood of Zacharias son of Barachias, whom ye slew between the temple and the altar." [Matthew 23:35]*

The phrase, *"in the law of Moses, and in the prophets, and in the psalms"* is the TaNaK. These passages undeniably denote the tripartite division of the TaNaK of the Jews by Jesus **and** the arrangement of the books of the Old Testament COS by the **Jews.**[9] The COS of the OT was not influenced or determined by the cultic Essenes at Qumran or by the racially mixed Samaritans (Rom. 3:1-2).

---

[8] Dr. W. W. Klein, Dr. Craig L. Blomberg, Dr. R. L. Hubbard, Jr., *Introduction To Biblical Interpretation* (W. Publishing Group, Thomas Nelson, Nashville, TN., 1993) p. 57.
[9] Strouse, Dr. Thomas M.; *The Lord Have Spoken: A Guide To Bibliology;* Emmanuel Baptist Theological Press; Newington, CT; 1998, p. 44, 38-50.

Furthermore, Jesus repeatedly said, *"It is written..."* He was referring to the Jewish TaNak. This also contravenes and contradicts the use of the Dead Sea Scrolls to correct, change, subtract, add to, or support in any way the scholars who give undue authority to the DSS.

Suppositions

The statement noted above in the book, *The Canon Debate*, concerning the synod at Jamnia, was preceded by the authors evidence, which included many words such as "probably," "seems," (claims of) "additions," "implies," "perhaps," etc. This is the norm in allegedly scholarly works today. One author literally excused the fabricated Synod of Jamnia theory by using many of the "conditional" terms above. He said:

> "Confronted...with Ryle's "we happen to know," it is only natural that the reading public would assume that Ryle's assertions rested on definite texts (though he sites none). Scholars are **perhaps** to be **excused** for their overlooking the uncertainty expressed in Ryle's next paragraph with the words "may," "apparently," "conjecture," and "symbolize."[10] [my emphasis]

H. E. Ryle popularized the Jamnia theory.

Scholars and Philosophy

Scholarolatry, like the worship of Mary, called Mariolatry, is discussed at length in this work because the worship of scholars, which was rampant in modernism, is still prevalent today, although postmodernists deny its continuation. However, postmodernists also worship the 'new' philosophical position of postmodernism which is a

---

[10] Jack P. Lewis, *The Canon Debate*, op. cit.; pp. 147-148.

man-made philosophy intellectually created by scholars. There are repeated warnings in Scripture about the philosophical traditions of men (cf. Col. 2:8). Even so, today, postmodern ideas constructed by scholars supplant Scripture.[11] Moreover, scholars forgive or excuse each other for proclaiming suppositions and false statements to be truth. The worship of scholars is prevalent today as never before. It is the reason one scholar *forgives* or excuses another for proclaiming false statements as truth. This is the 'new' tolerance. Political correctness allows the scholar to make whatever theory he concocts to be considered true. In postmodernism, this tendency is extending to the man on the street. In the name of tolerance, no idea invented by any person is wrong. In addition, it should not be challenged because, for that person and his experiences, it may be true.

We could spend literally thousands of pages discussing the false THEORIES of men such as Thomas Hobbes, Bernard Spinoza, F. C. Baur, Julius Wellhausen, Adolf von Harnack, Herman Gunkle, Karl Barth, Rudolf Bultman, B. S. Childs, H. von Campenhausen, A. C. Sundberg, H. Y. Gamble, L. M. McDonald, James A. Sanders, Bart Ehrman, etc. In addition, thousands of pages could be spent on the influence of hermeneutical approaches to Scripture and their relation to the COS such as:

1. Rabbinic Judaism,
2. *Halakah* (Heb. "rule to go by"),
3. *Haggadah* (Heb. "a telling"), or
4. *Pesher,* an inspired application of the Hebrew prophecies to historical events of the end time from Dan. 4:16. It is associated with the Qumran (Essene) community, or

---

[11] H. D. Williams, M.D., Ph.D., *Hearing the Voice of God* (The Old Paths Publications, Cleveland, GA, 2008) Chapter 6.

5. patristic hermeneutics, particularly from Alexandrian Church elders, or
6. scholasticism, or
7. the Reformation, or
8. rationalism, or
9. the historical-critical method, or
10. source criticism, or
11. form criticism, or
12. kerygma, or
13. redaction criticism, etc.

However, the scope of this work is to address only the latest method of attack on the COS and the inscripturated Words.

The New Academic Course: "Canon Criticism"

The newest approach, called *Canon Criticism*[12] is exacting a toll on our generation, because of the *debate* it has spawned. *Canon Criticism* is a postgraduate academic course at a number of schools. The tenets of humanistic and rationalist literary structuralism, deconstructionism, feminism, and liberation theology included in the course work, have freed the postmodern "whatever" generation to use a *"pen-knife"* on the books of Scripture without hesitation. It leads to claiming there are many false canonical books and "proto-orthodox" inserts or additions to the Words in the COS.

---

[12] Klein, op. cit., p. 51 (*Introduction to Biblical Interpretation*). Many are promoting *Canon Criticism* as an improvement of previous hermeneutical approaches to Scripture; however, close examination reveals only a 'softening' of the harsh criticism of the *received* COS.

The attempt to use a pen-knife on the Scripture to destroy its integrity is not new. The same "seed of apostasy" infected King Jehoiakim and caused him to cut up Jeremiah's scroll that contained God's Words. They were the Words given to Jeremiah by God to be recorded by his amanuensis, Baruch (see Jer. 36).

The same "seed of apostasy" is present today. Modernistic and postmodernistic "scholars" fertilize and water the seed with their philosophies and theories. This author is convinced that the growth of this "seed of apostasy" is leading to the curse of Mal. 4:6, Hos. 4:6, and Psa. 106:27 as explained later in this presentation.

The Shift in the Attack by Canon Criticism

Lastly, the paradigm shift in the attack on the Scriptures is widespread. The assault has changed from attacking the **Words** of the Traditional Greek Text (TT) or Received Greek Text (RT) to **Canon criticism** by the advocates of the recently formulated academic discipline.[13] This prototype shift has occurred for several reasons. (1) Previous attacks on the Words have been thwarted because of the demonstration of the existence of the early TT and (2) because of strong defenders of its apostolic origin.[14] There is an organization called the Dean Burgon Society, to which this author belongs, whose members defend the origin and transmission of the text.[15] **The modern critical text advocates and enemies of the TT,**

---

[13] Ibid. p. 53ff.
[14] Dr. Jack Moorman, *Early Church Fathers and the Authorized Version, A Demonstration* (Bible For Today Press, Collingswood, NJ, BFT # 2136) pp. 1-38. This has been release in hardback as: *Early Manuscripts, Church Fathers, and the Authorized Version.* 2005. BFT #3230BK.
[15] Dean Burgon Society, www.deanburgonsociety.org.

recognizing their Antiochian and Lucian recension theories as well as their critical text theories have been dispelled,[16] had to find another way to discredit the TT in order to salvage their attack on the Scriptures. T*heir (re)construction of the critical text by textual criticism cannot be defended*. Therefore, their current method is:

1. to attack the very books of the *received* COS as frauds,
2. to propose an open canon,
3. to recommend discarded Gnostic books or spurious pseudonymous (falsely named authors) books to the COS, and
4. to claim large passages in Scripture are additions or inserts in the TT.

This redirection of the postmodern attack from the Words to the Canon has gathered steam since the early 1990's. Scholarolatry is contributing to the shift from discrediting the "jots and tittles" to attempting to discredit the COS. Hopefully, this limited work will bolster the confidence of believers and understanding will be enhanced by a look at the new direction the enemy is taking. Rest assured, believers have the COS that was intended for NT saints to receive.

---

[16] Williams, M. D., H. D.; *The Lie That Changed The Modern World* (Bible For Today Press, Collingswood, NJ; 2004) p. 215. Even Kurt Aland and K. W. Clark agree that the "age of Westcott and Hort" is over.

CHAPTER 1

WHAT IS THE CANON OF SCRIPTURE?

"But we will not boast of things without our measure, but according to the measure of **the rule** *which God hath distributed to us, a measure to reach even unto you" (2 Cor. 10:13)*

What is the Canon of Scripture (COS)? The word, canon, is from the Hebrew word, קָנֶה, qaneh, and the Greek word, κανον, kanon, meaning rule, pen, reed, or rod to measure by. Careful exegesis and interpretation of certain biblical passages define the Canon of Scripture for us. It is **God's inspired canonical Words** in 66 books[17] that are inscripturated in Hebrew, Aramaic, and Greek. The Words are "the way of life," and they are protective. They are the "rule" man should use to serve God and other men. The Words are arranged into books as different authors recorded the Words. The contractual Words were given as the rule of faith [2 Cor. 2:13-15, Gal. 6:16, Philip. 3:16], the rule of truth, [Heb. 13:17, Jn. 17:17], and the rule of practice [2 John 1:6, 3 John 1:4, 1 John 1:7, Eph. 5:8, 1 Thess. 4:1]. The Words cannot be added to, subtracted from, or changed in word order, spelling, or jots and tittles (letters) (Rev. 22:18, Deut. 4:2). The everlasting God commanded that the Words of the Canon of Scripture are to be *"made known to all nations for the obedience to the faith"* [Rom 16:25-26, 1

---

[17] Strouse, Dr. Thomas M.; op. cit., p. 70 (*The Lord Hath Spoken*).

Cor. 14:21], which means that the original words received in Hebrew, Aramaic, and Greek were to be translated into other languages.

The KJB is The Canon Preserved in English

The KJB is the preserved canon, rule, or measure of Scripture in English because it meets the following requirements outlined so well for us in 1999 by Dr. Robert J. Barnett, a member of the Executive Committee and Vice-president of the Dean Burgon Society. He reports that Turretin said:

> "The Scriptures are called canonical for a double reason, both with regard to the doctrines (because they are the canon and standard of faith and practice, derived from the Hebrew QNH, which signifies a "reed" or surveyor's pen and is so used in Gal. 6:16 and Phil 3:16) and with respect to the books (because it contains all the canonical books)." The KJB can be called our English canon and standard of faith and practice only if we claim that all such doctrinal authority within the KJB is derived from its own underlying Hebrew, Aramaic, and Greek text.
> "Only because all 66 books of the Old and New Testament, and all the traditional verses, phrases, and words within those 66 books are accurately translated into the KJB can it be considered our English canon and standard of faith and practice."[18] (This rules out all other modern Bible versions in English.)

Accurate and faithful translations (AFTs) of the pure, preserved, perfect Words of God are rare today. Nevertheless, progress

---

[18] Dr. Robert J. Barnett, "The King James Bible Authority" (The Dean Burgon Society Messages, From the 22nd Annual Meeting ,#10 in a series, Bible For Today #2999-P Collingswood, NJ, July 19-20, 1999) p. 8.

Chapter 1: What is the Canon of Scripture?

is being made around the world by a few faithful men to remedy the situation. As Turretin said:

> "**Unless unimpaired integrity characterize the Scriptures, they could not be regarded as the sole rule of faith and practice,** and the door would be thrown wide open to atheists, libertines, enthusiasts and other profane persons like them for destroying its authenticity (authentian) and overthrowing the foundation of salvation. For since nothing false can be an object of faith, how could the Scriptures be held as authentic and reckoned divine if liable to contradictions...For if **once the authenticity (authentia) of Scriptures is taken away (which would result even from the incurable corruption of one passage), how could our faith rest on what remains?** And **if corruption is admitted in those of lesser importance, why not in others of greater?**"[19]

The COS is Mentioned in Scripture

This author could not find a better concept related to the Canon (rule) of Scripture, although he searched everywhere. The Scripture says,

> "But we will not boast of things without our measure, but according to the measure of **the rule** [Gr. kanon] which God hath distributed to us, a measure to reach even unto you." [2 Cor. 10:13]

> And as many as walk according to **this rule**, [Gr. kanon] peace be on them, and mercy, and upon the Israel of God. [Galatians 6:16]

> Nevertheless, whereto we have already attained, let us walk by the **same rule**, [Gr. kanon] let us mind the same thing. [Philip. 3:16]

---

[19] Ibid. p. 8. (Barnett, "The King James Bible Authority").

The word, canon,[20] is applied to:

"the Scriptures, [THE WORDS] to denote that they contained the authoritative rule of faith and practice, the standard of doctrine and duty. A book is said to be of canonical authority when it has a right to take a place with the other books which contain a revelation of the Divine will. Such a right does not arise from any ecclesiastical authority, but from the evidence of the inspired authorship of the book. The canonical (i.e., the inspired) books of the Old and New Testaments, are a complete rule, and the only rule, of faith and practice. They contain the whole supernatural revelation of God to men."[21] [My addition, HDW]

The Way of Life Encyclopedia states:

"The Lord Jesus Christ promised that the Holy Spirit would guide the Christians "into all truth" [THE WORDS] (Jn 16:7-6:43). The epistle of 1 John also promises that the Holy Spirit will guide the believers in the truth. It is the Holy Spirit who taught the sincere Christians to accept the New Testament Scripture and to reject everything that was erroneous. Our confidence in this matter is not in men, but in God who has given us these promises."[22] [my addition, HDW]

The COS is the measure (rule) that reaches to you. If it has not reached you presently, by the Lord's decree, there is coming a day when it will (Jn. 12:47-48, Rev. 20:12).

---

[20] The word canon by itself may imply the canon (rule or measure) of architecture, philosophy, sculpture, law, etc.
[21] Easton, *Easton's 1897 Bible Dictionary,* Wordsearch, iExalt Electronic Publishing; Austin, TX; Version 5.K; Canon.
[22] David W. Cloud, *Way of Life Encyclopedia of the Bible and Christianity, 4th Edition;* Way of Life Literature, Port Huron, MI, 2002, p. 93.

The Mistake of Naturalistic Textual Critics

Many individuals are perplexed by the *mechanisms* for establishment[23] of the Canon of Scripture. It is not difficult. *"He that is of God heareth God's words."* Wilbur Pickering's book, *The Identity of the New Testament Text*,[24] contains excellent material related to this topic. Dr Pickering speaks about the confusion of naturalistic textual critic scholars[25] concerning when and how the New Testament writings

---

[23] Jay P. Green, *Unholy Hands on the Bible;* Vol. II (Sovereign Grace Trust Fund, Lafayette, IN, 1992) pp. 412ff. See this reference for another presentation of the establishment and preservation of the Canon of Scripture.
[24] Wilbur Pickering, *The Identity of the New Testament Text]* (Thomas Nelson Publishers, Nashville, TN, 1980) This book is excellent. However, Pastor Gary E. LaMore, Ph.D., D.D. has appropriately called our attention to W. Pickering's surprise ending and his Majority Text penchant. Please see the *DBS Message Book,* #13, pp. 11-64.
[25] The *critical text* **'scholars'** (most humble Bible-believers call themselves *students* of God's words) have blurred the issues by insisting on a **list** of canonical writings as the definition of the word, canon. In this fashion, they may contend that no early **list** of canonical books has been found because the books of Scripture were not established and were contested. [See *The Canon Debate*, p. 11; *The Canon of Scripture,* p. 18] Rather, the proper view should be that canonical books were recognized as Scripture immediately by most [See *The Text of the New Testament*, p. 100f], and that some other books, as the *Shepherd of Hermas,* were highly regarded, but they came not to be included in the canon of Scripture by the guidance of the Holy Spirit. Why was there a need for a **list** if communications between regions were excellent [p. 107, *The Identity of the New Testament Text*], essentially everyone knew which were the canonical books for sure, only a few churches or individuals considered other books canonical, they had copies of the canonical books, they knew where the originals were (see Strouse, *The Lord Hath Spoken,* p. 72); and the 'world' population was small? In spite of what we are often told, even Revelation was considered canonical immediately. [p. 104, *The Identity of the New Testament Text]* The view of the *critical text* 'scholars' demanding a list would be similar to someone needing a list

were ***recognized*** and transmitted as books of the sacred Canon. He relates that the infamous J. F. A. Hort said:

> "Textual purity, as far as can be judged from the extant literature, attracted hardly any interest. There is no evidence to show that care was generally taken to choose out for transcription the exemplars having the highest claims to be regarded as authentic, if indeed the requisite knowledge and skill were forthcoming."[26] [my emphasis, HDW]

Pickering also relates E. C. Colwell as saying:

> "Most of the manuals and handbooks now in print (including mine!) will tell you that these variations were the fruit of careless treatment which was possible because **the books of the New Testament had not yet attained a strong position as "Bible."**[27] [my emphasis, not my words in the parentheses, HDW]

As usual, the *critical text* proponents ignore, shade, or lie about the proclamations of a living God and the known history of the text. The Words of God were ***immediately recognized*** as canonical Words that were to be placed into the COS. [cf. 1 Cor. 14:37, 2 Cor. 10:1-16, (v. 13 contains G. kanon); Gal. 1:6-12; 2 Thess. 3:6-14, 2 Pet. 3:2, 15-16; 1 Tim. 5:18, Luke and Deuteronomy are called Scripture by Paul].[28] Many places in the NT reveal that the Words recorded by King David were the inspired Words of the Holy Spirit (cf. Heb. 4:7).

---

of TV stations in an area where he lives. **Any child would know without a list.**
[26] Wilbur Pickering, *The Identity of the New Testament Text* (Thomas Nelson Publishers, Nashville, TN, 1980) p. 100.
[27] Ibid. p. 100.
[28] The "scholars" proclaim that the Church "created" the canon. The truth is they ***recognized*** it.

Chapter 1: What is the Canon of Scripture?

The Apostles and prophets knew when they were receiving Words from the Holy Spirit and when they were to record the Words[29] from God that would become the inscripturated Words (1 Cor. 2:4, 12-13). Some discerning Bible-believers think that the Holy Spirit actually dictated the words.[30] Pickering comments on Justin Martyr's (ca. 100/114-ca. 162/168) *Dialogue with Trypho*. He said Justin Martyr:

> "shows a masterful knowledge of the Old Testament to which he assigns the highest possible authority, evidently holding to a dictation view of inspiration—in *Trypho 34* he says, 'to persuade you that you have not understood anything of the Scriptures, I will remind you of another psalm, <u>dictated</u> to David by the Holy Spirit"[31] [my emphasis]

King David affirms this concept in 1 Chron. 28:19 when he says,

> *All this, said David, the* **Lord made me understand in writing by his hand upon me,** *even all the works of this pattern. [Also, see 1 Pe. 1:21]*

However, did the Holy Spirit dictate evil letters such as the evil letter dictated by David (cf. 2 Sam. 11:14-15)? Of course not, but He insured that they would be included for our learning (1 Cor. 10:6). The exact mechanism of determining the Words to be inscripturated will never be understood on this side of heaven. As stated in the preface of this work, the sacred mystery of inscripturation of the Words of canonical books is not understood perfectly. But, the mechanism will

---

[29] Strouse, op. cit., pp. 44-50. (*The Lord Hath Spoken*).
[30] Cloud, David, D.D., *The Way of Life Encyclopedia of the Bible and Christianity*, (Way of Life Literature, Port Huron, MI; 2002) p. 299. Dr. Strouse does not agree with this position. See p. 45, *The Lord Hath Spoken*.
[31] Ibid. pp. 103-104.

be understood sufficiently enough to accept the doctrines concerning God's Words found in His Holy Book.

Wilbur Pickering's description of the history of the text, or in other words, the history of the church receiving the canonical words or books of the Bible, is superb and should be read by everyone, including the *critical text* supporters.[32]

The Attack on the COS Uncovered

The interest in the Canon of Scripture by so many of the postmodernists does not fool anyone. Since the rationalists and *critical text* proponents realize that they cannot get rid of the Received Text (TT/RT) by claiming Lucianic recensions and denying its early existence, they have to find other ways to discredit the RT or Traditional Text. Specifically, they have to call into question their existence:

1. by calling the canonical books frauds or,

---

[32] Pickering, op. cit., pp. 99-120 (*The Identity of the New Testament Text*). However, one should be aware of Pickering's penchant for the Majority Text (this is the name formerly given to the Received Text by some authors, but is a corrupted word, and Majority Text is now used for yet a 'new' text), which neither this author *nor* the Dean Burgon Society supports. Dr. Robert J. Barnett says, "One should also consult Dr. Hills [who] represented an important 20th century link in the contingency which unites us with Burgon, Owen, Beza and other giants in each generation of an unbroken line, going back to the original infallible autographs. - Believing Bible Study, pp. 194-205. Dr. Hills defended the old KJB not as just another good translation, but as representative of an established standard or **canon** of Holy Scriptures which we in the 20th century have no divine right or authority to replace. ["Dr. Edward Freer Hills' Position on The King James Bible," The Dean Burgon Society's 1991 Meeting, by Dr. Robert Barnett, Vice President of the Dean Burgon Society, 1991 Message Book] Also, see Dr. Gary L. LaMore's, "Wilbur Pickering's Surprise Ending", DBS Message Book, 2003.

2. by casting doubt about the mechanism for acceptance of the books or epistles as canonical, God-breathed books by the early church.

Additionally, this author is not convinced that all ante-Nicene Church elders used apograph manuscripts from the Alexandrian (CT) corrupt route as is alleged by most CT proponents. Why? One must apply the following considerations:

1. First, only Alexandrians (*CT proponents*) proclaim that the *critical text-type* manuscripts:
    a. are the "oldest and best," and
    b. are the MSS quoted **primarily** by ante-Nicene church elders.
2. Secondly, their assertion that these manuscripts were the "proto" or closest to the original manuscripts cannot be sustained or proven.
3. Thirdly, the CT men never point out that even though the Alexandrian texts were quoted by the early Church elders, the quotes may have been misquotes, quotes by heretics or apostates, or quotes by orthodox defenders of the faith of heretics to refute them. Most importantly, they NEVER point out the significantly **fewer** quotes of the assumed "oldest and best" manuscripts.

Conservative Researcher's Evidence

However, Bible-believing conservative researchers, such as Dr. Jack Moorman, have demonstrated several very important and key facts.

1. First, the early Church elders quoted from the Traditional Text (Received Text) or canon MUCH more frequently than they quoted from texts **that could be considered** Alexandrian.[33]
2. Secondly, the Alexandrian Texts or manuscripts, which total only **1.0%** of preserved manuscripts, do not agree. In other words, few if *any* two verses in those **1.0%** of manuscripts agree. The MSS are not the same and differ in many aspects.
3. Thirdly therefore, the "misquotes" by the early Church elders may well have occurred because of three factors:

    a. The Church elder may not have retrieved his valuable, precious, costly, fragile manuscripts out of storage. Subsequently, he may have quoted the verse incorrectly. Have you ever quoted a verse incorrectly? This author has many times. On occasions, it is very embarrassing.

    b. An ancient church elder as an apologetic defense against heretics may quote incorrectly a verse because the heretics quoted it incorrectly. Perhaps, a much closer examination of quotes by church elders by an excellent non-biased linguist and student should be undertaken. However, the work would take a lifetime because of the extensive knowledge needed, much less the time and money.

---

[33] Moorman, Dr. Jack A., *Early Church Fathers and the Authorized Version A Demonstration* (Bible For Today Press, Collingswood, NJ, B.F.T. #2136, 2005).

c. Lastly, many quotes that favor the CT or Alexandrian type manuscripts are those made by known apostates and heretics.

The extreme *non-agreement* of all Alexandrian texts is significant, and therefore, calls into question the "quoting" of the alleged "oldest and best" Alexandrian text-type MSS by Church elders. The most popular "oldest and best" text-types are also known as the Sinaiticus or Aleph MS, Vaticanus or B manuscript MS, Alexandrinus MS, Beza MS, and D MS. If possible, the church elders quotes should be correlated to determine whether they are an exact quote of the Alexandrian text or whether the Alexandrian quote was used by a writer to point out heretics' corruption of the text.

It is also distressing that a recent book, *The Canon Debate*, released in 2002, spends many pages **debating**:

1. the meaning of the word, canon,

2. what comprises the Canon of Scripture,

3. how the Canon came about, and

4. what authority established the Canon of Scripture.

In light of Scripture, these questions asked by liberal naturalistic textual critics and scholars are moot.

CHAPTER 2

SCHOLAROLATRY

"He that is of God heareth God's words: ye therefore hear them not, because ye are not of God" John 8:47

Scholars Using Scholarolatry

We will evaluate the book, *Canon Debate,* and another, *Lost Christianities,* which have attacked God's Words or His Canon by suppositions, assumptions, theories, and guesses. These authors have written numerous books.[34] Not all of their books or every fact can be addressed. Rather, a broad look at their assumptions will be addressed.

Frequently, scholars accept their proposed hypotheses as facts as they worship one another and as others worship them. This is called scholarolatry. Moreover, they confuse issues by redefining concepts and terms. For example, the editors of the book, *The Canon Debate,* contend that a canonical book must be able to:

> "be adapted to new circumstances of life or it ceases to be canonical."[35]

and

> "Relevance or adaptability has always been the primary trait of a canon, early and late."[36]

---

[34] Such as Bart D. Ehrman's *Misquoting Jesus, The Da Vinci Code, Lost Scriptures,* etc. published by Oxford University Press, NY.
[35] McDonald, op. cit. p. 10 (*The Canon Debate*).
[36] Ibid. p. 259.

This is contrary to all the doctrines of the Scriptures. The "Book" must *not* be able to adapt to man, but in God's eyes, man *must* be able to *adapt* to the "Book," which is His fixed unchangeable covenant with man. Sadly, man has not accomplished this feat in any dispensation. Man has consistently failed to come under the authority of the Almighty God in every dispensation.

These men should review all uses of the Hebrew words, shâmar and nâtsar, and the Greek words, τηρεω and εκκλεσια in Scripture. The fixity of Scripture will be discovered. Alternatively, reading *Thou Shalt Keep Them*, Kent Brandenburg, Editor, from Pillar and Ground Publishing would help anyone to understand the issue.

From the definition of a canonical book given by the editors of *The Canon Debate,* any orthodox canonical book:

1. that does not conform to man's ideas or
2. that is offensive to a denomination or
3. that is not adaptable, such as the apocalyptic book of Revelation, may be removed.

And yes, this is exactly what they recommend.[37] The editors of *The Canon Debate* list almost three dozen scholars who use their theories to proclaim an unsettled open Canon of Scripture. Many individuals accept their proclamations because of scholarolatry. Scholarolatry leads individuals to accept false statements as facts or assumptions as truth. Scholars dupe unsuspecting readers, hearers, or listeners by their seats of authority and by lauding defective scholarship, as was demonstrated above. Our children are taught to worship academics as opposed to giving them appropriate respect. Whatever has happened to the use of the words, "This is only my opinion and it may not be correct." in a scholarly book?

---

[37] Ibid. p. 3.

Dr. Waite, President of the DBS, reported in 1985:

> One of our DBS Vice Presidents, Dr. David Otis Fuller, uses the expression 'scholarolatry.'[38]

I recently asked Dr. Waite if it (scholarolatry) is worse today. He said:

> "I would answer that SCHOLAROLATRY is just as great if not greater in the days in which we live than in 1985. One evidence of this is that in BOTH of the recent anti-textus receptus and anti-preservation of the Hebrew and Greek **Words** books sponsored by Bob Jones University graduates and friends make use of a group of men that they call the "ACADEMICIANS" who have looked over their work and made suggestions. The "ACADEMICIANS" were listed in both [books] FROM THE MIND OF GOD TO THE MIND OF MAN (with 8 "Dr's" from seven schools and one mission board in 1999) and in GOD'S WORD IN OUR HANDS (with 10 "Dr's" from nine schools in 2003). You can't convince me that these ACADEMICIANS were just listed for the fun of it. I firmly believe that they were listed to bolster the many false statements appearing within these books and to make unsuspecting lay people, and others, believe these false statements to be true statements because of SCHOLAROLATRY, the worship of so-called "scholarship," even if it is FALSE "scholarship."[39] [my addition, HDW]

Protecting Our Children From "Scholarolatry"

It is also distressing to many of us that most of the authors of the books mentioned above are professors and teachers of our children in this nation and other nations around the world. They have enormous influence on thousands of students in universities, Bible

---

[38] *The Dean Burgon Society News*, May-August, 1985, pages 2-4.
[39] Personal communication to this author by Dr. Waite on June 6, 2004 via email.

colleges, and seminaries. Our concern relates to these men and women:

1. attacking the very foundations of our culture,
2. weakening the moral fabric of the world, and
3. ***confusing*** our children by casting doubt on the preserved Hebrew, Aramaic, and Greek words of Scripture by employing scholarolatry.

In my opinion, the writings by these "scholars," who seem to take no account of their responsibilities, must be answered. Their written pronouncements in their books, based on argumentum ad hominem attacks on the greatest piece of literature to ever grace this world, must be challenged. They must be called to accountability. Their philosophy of life, their traditions, their banal statements, their conjectures, and their disregard for the Truth [John 17:17] must not be left unchallenged, expecting our innocent children to sort things out. The seriousness of the attack on the Canon of Scripture by pedantic modern scholars is as serious as the folly of Westcott and Hort, along with their associates and friends, who concocted a false Greek text.[40]

---

[40] Dean John William Burgon, *The Revision Revised* (The Dean Burgon Society Press, Collingswood, NJ, originally published 1880's, republished 2000, 2nd printing). This book is an amazing exposé of Westcott and Hort's folly.

CHAPTER 3

GOD'S YOUNG MESSENGER WARNS "SCHOLARS"

"Beware lest any man spoil you through philosophy and vain deceit, after the tradition of men, after the rudiments of the world, and not after Christ" Colossians 2:8

Scholars are warned repeatedly in the Scriptures. In an account described in the book of Job, chapters 31 and following, Job replies to the scourging words from his three friends, Eliphaz, Bildad, and Zophar. Job's answer to his friends is peppered with I, me, myself, and mine, appearing some 80 times in 40 verses in chapter 31. Next, Elihu, the young preacher, appears on the scene.[41] His words display significant displeasure towards Job. Apparently, it is because Job justified himself instead of God. Over the next six chapters, the young preacher takes his turn upbraiding Job.

Some of the wise comments by Elihu will be presented. He is obviously a herald of God sent to Job. His explanations to Job have application to scholars who depend on scholarolatry and who are allegedly "great" and "wise" and perhaps "aged" men. Then we will examine a statement to Job by God about the ostrich, which has application to scholars who are responsible for the education of **millions** of students.

---

[41] Note that God did not require an offering for the young preacher, Elihu, as God did for Job's three friends, Eliphaz, Bildad, and Zophar. (See Job 42:7-10).

The Inspiration of the Almighty

Elihu, the young preacher, asserts a man must be attuned to *"the inspiration of the Almighty"* to have understanding. What is *"the inspiration of the Almighty"*? It is the inspired Words of God. Paul said:

> *"All scripture is given by inspiration of God, and is profitable for doctrine, for reproof, for correction, for instruction in righteousness" 2 Timothy 3:16.*

A man called *"great,"* or *"wise"* by the world does not mean he understands *"judgment,"* that is, *"the inspiration of the Almighty."* Elihu says:

> *But there is a spirit in man: and* **the inspiration of the Almighty** *giveth them understanding.* **Great** *men are not always* **wise**: *neither do the* **aged** *understand judgment. [Job 32:8-9]*

Elihu warns us about a man who is *called* "great" and "wise." He affirms that the spirit of a man or the age of a man is no guarantee of understanding the Scripture. Elihu makes it clear that the scholar is not always right. Only God is to be worshipped (Ex. 20:1-6, 34:14, Mat. 4:10).

Inductively, **all** the Words of God give wisdom, not just those words or books *chosen* by scholars as Scripture. [2 Tim 3:16, 2 Pe 1:21, John 3:3-8, Prov. 1, 2, 3, 8, 9, 10]. Remember, they want to remove some books and claim false insertions into other books. They do not understand the "scarlet thread." Additionally, one must be *"born again"* to receive and understand *"the inspiration of the Almighty"* because the Holy Spirit *"giveth them understanding."*

One of the authors in *The Canon Debate,* James A. Sanders, proclaims in another article in a journal:

> "Some Christians embrace the idea from Greco—Roman mystery cults that entering the new family in Christ was like being "born again", or experiencing a new birth (an individual renaissance), which gave a totally new identity to anyone who embraced it."[42]

This author hopes this is not Sanders position. It would be wise for anyone holding to a similar thought, as noted in this quote, to read chapter three of the Gospel of John very carefully. Simply entering a "new family," such as an assembly of people, does not confer "a new birth." One must repent of his sins and believe God with all His heart.

Many individuals would say the section in John's Gospel is "probably" an insert by a member of a mystery cult even though lectionaries, translations into other languages, quotes by early Church elders and the testimony of thousands [including myself] support the reality of the Lord Jesus Christ's comments in chapter three. To interject their position and philosophy, they would point out that the Gnostics believed they held secret knowledge that led to salvation.

The young preacher Elihu says that even if God emphasizes a passage by repeating it twice, an unbeliever will not distinguish the truth by the *"spirit of man."* Elihu says,

> *For God speaketh once, yea twice, yet man perceiveth it not. [Job 33:14]*

---

[42] James A. Sanders, "The Family in the Bible" *(Biblical Theology Bulletin,* Seton Hall University, South Orange, NJ, Fall 2002) p. 6. The Bulletin is online at http://academic.shu.edu/btb/.

There are many concepts repeated many times in the Scriptures, yet many men do not perceive them.[43] Prayerfully, certain men will understand and perceive, by the end of this presentation, what they have done and are doing:

1. to the foundations of Scripture,
2. to the foundations of America and other nations, and
3. to the foundations of our families.

Perhaps they will also understand and perceive what they have done, in particular, to our children.

> "In fact, national surveys indicate that up to **51 percent** of **Christian** students no longer claim to be "born again" by their senior year in college."[44]

Finally, perhaps they will perceive **the results** that have emanated from their attack upon the plenarily and verbally preserved, pure, infallible, and inerrant Canon of Scripture reported later in this work.

Scholars Are Like The Ostrich

Returning to our story, after the young preacher Elihu finishes with his chastisement of Job, God tells Job to, *"Gird up now thy loins like a man for I will demand of thee, and answer thou me."* [Job 38:3]. Then God gives Job a list of questions that are still unanswerable by "great" and "wise" men.

---

[43] Sanders, *The Family in the Bible;* Biblical theology Bulletin, Fall, 2002, says, "Hiding homophobia behind five scattered biblical verses is devious in the extreme" This is an example of man not "perceiving" the truth. Homosexualism causes a 40–50 % shorter life span. In love Christians try to save their lives, and would even if there were only one verse; H. D. Williams, M.D., Ph.D.

[44] Please see Appendix 4.

Present day "scholars" cannot answer God's questions either. Too many are very pompous. Science, logic, or philosophy will never answer the important questions in life. Look how often each discipline has changed facts, thoughts, and ideas, which at times had been considered absolute, over the last six thousand years (e.g. the earth is flat, there is no matter smaller than an atom). Many men in these academic fields remind us of God's description of an ostrich. In chapter 39, verses 14-17, God describes some of the characteristics of an ostrich:

> *"Which leaveth her eggs in the earth, and warmeth them in dust, ¹⁵And forgetteth that the foot may crush them, or that the wild beast may break them. ¹⁶* **She is hardened against her young ones***, as though they were not hers: her labour is in vain without fear; ¹⁷Because God hath deprived her of wisdom, neither hath he imparted to her understanding. [Job 39:14-17]*

The fear of many lovers of God's Words is that many so-called *"great"* and *"wise"* men do not have the Spirit of God and they *"darkeneth counsel by words without knowledge"* of the pure and perfect Truth (Job 32:8-9, 38:2). They are deprived of wisdom because they reject God's providentially preserved Words that He said **He** would preserve. [Psa 12:6-7, Mat. 24:35, 1 Pe. 1:23-25]

Their concept of "love" is tolerance, without judging or speaking out against ideas contrary to absolute Truth. They believe love is God.[45] They appear to have no concept of an omniscient, omnipotent, omnipresent God who inhabits eternity and who judges

---

[45] "God is love," 1 Jn 4:8, (not the other way around) and "whoso keepeth (τηρεω, guards, keeps, preserves, obeys) His **word** in him verily is the love **of** God perfected" [1 John 2:5]. Until a "scholar" can understand these two verses, he is in trouble.

evil. [Isa. 57:15-21] Like an ostrich, they do *not* perceive danger; the danger of their pronouncements to our children, to our families, and to our nations.

These scholars, who are rejecting Truth, are unleashing a torrent of violence and licentious behavior by releasing depraved man from a firm foundation [Isa. 1:5-6, 28:16, 53:6, 1 Cor. 3:10-12]. They probably have **no** idea that they are contributing to this "curse" (see Appendix 8). They do not understand that they are undermining the very foundation of Truth: faith in the incomprehensible God and "the fruit of His lips," His Words to man (Isa. 57:19). God gave the Words to protect mankind.[46] [John 17:17, Psa 11:3, Isa. 51:12, Lk 6:48-49, 1Co. 3:11, Eph. 2:20, 2 Tim. 2:19, Lk 17:2] Scholars discouragement of young people particularly is causing irreparable harm. If they *perceive* the danger, they are callously ignoring it.

In my opinion, in their insatiable desire to uncover something academically startling, astonishing, and new for publishing, they have crossed the line of decency, honor, and respect. They have exalted "self" and their false idea of "love (tolerance)" above the common good, and more seriously, above the Scriptures, the very Words of a living God. Like the ostrich, they have stuck their heads into the ground. They are oblivious to the dangers threatening them and their children.

---

[46] God's pleas throughout the Scriptures are for man to comprehend, obey, keep, protect, guard, and preserve His "jots and tittles." They are given for the protection of man spiritually and physically. [Prov. 3:8] For example, before man understood that disease came from microbes, God instituted protective measures against them. [Lev, 13, 15, 16, e. g. Lev. 13:6, and many other places] Before man understood spiritual dangers, God instituted protective measures. [Deut. 18:10, Mic 5:12] The Truth [John 17:17] is given for protection, which leads to the ultimate protection, salvation and eternal life.

What Have The Scholars Done?

What have the scholars done? The question is answered by a look back, a survey of the attack on the Canon of Scripture by *"great men [who] are not always wise,"* [Job 32:9] and then by an examination of the same errors made today that were made millenniums ago. The Scripture records many instances of the assault on *"the everlasting covenant,"* which is the Old Testament and the New Testament.[47] We will *briefly* examine a few of those attacks in the following order:

1. The Old Testament's record of the assault on the Canon of Scripture, and
2. The New Testament's *comments* on the attack of Scripture.

This will be followed by a short review of the assault on the Canon of Scripture since the incarnation of our Lord Jesus Christ. It will be broken into four headings:

3. The attack on the Canon in the first three centuries,
4. The present day "scholars" follies revealed within their trite academic works, which assault the very Words of God and His canon,
5. The Scripture speaks, and finally,
6. The Conclusion.

---

[47] This author realizes there are many ways to exegete "the everlasting covenant" in Scripture. It can refer to the Davidic Covenant, the New Covenant, the Lord Jesus Christ, the entire Bible (OT and NT), etc.

CHAPTER 4

THE ASSAULT ON THE OLD TESTAMENT CANON

"And he said unto them, These are the words which I spake unto you, while I was yet with you, that all things must be fulfilled, which were written in the law of Moses, and in the prophets, and in the psalms, concerning me"
Luke 24:44

In addition to the infamous attack on God's Words in the Garden [Gen 3:1-7], there are many other scenes depicted in the TaNak (Old Testament) related to preservation of the text against the "wiles" of apostasy and persecutions. Dr. Waite reports on these attacks. He said:

> "Apostasy and persecutions under Kings Ahaz, Manasseh, and Amon, plus [the] capture of Jerusalem by Nebuchadnezzar (606-586 B.C.), by Antiochus Ephiphanes, with the Maccabean persecutions (170-165 B.C.), and by Titus (70 A.D.); the results of revolt under Bar Cocha (132-135 A.D.); the persecutions under Roman Emperors, wars and troubles of various kinds—[during] many of these disasters, the Scriptures were ordered destroyed."[48] [my addition, HDW]

These attacks, other assaults, and the destruction of worn out manuscripts by scribes left future generations with only 1700 Old

---

[48] Dr. D. A. Waite, "How We Got Our Bible," DBS Website, p. 9 of 16, www.deanburgonsociety.org/howbible.htm.

Testament Hebrew and Aramaic manuscripts (MSS) as of 1960.[49] Of course "only 1700" is in reality many compared with the few copies of books like Homer's Iliad (700 MSS), Euripides plays (350 MSS), and *The Annals of Tacitus* (1 MS).[50]

One particular assault on the Canon recorded in the OT cannot be passed over because it reveals several important or key principles in this battle. It illustrates:
1. The inspiration of God's Words,
2. The preservation of God's Words by copies, and
3. The attack on the Canon by proud apostate men.

Attacks Thwarted by Copies of All His Words

The Words of Scripture tell the account better than this author obviously could, but a summary is offered here. In Jeremiah, chapter 36, Jeremiah was commanded to WRITE IN A BOOK, *"ALL THE WORDS THAT I [God] HAVE SPOKEN UNTO THEE."* The passage repeatedly emphasizes that *"ALL THE WORDS"* were written and *"ALL THE WORDS"* were read ON SEVERAL OCCASIONS. Eventually, *"ALL THE WORDS"* were read to the King of Judah, King Jehoiakim. The King immediately became a "scholar" and a mutilator of Scripture. The King used a PENKNIFE to cut up the book and, finally, he BURNED IT.

God is never outdone however, so He ordered Jeremiah (and therefore his amanuensis, Baruch the scribe) to make a copy. God said,

---

[49] Ibid. p. 9.
[50] Ehrman, op. cit., p 219 (*Lost Christianities*). Also, see and Bruce M. Metzger, *The New Testament, Its Background, Growth, and Content*, 3rd Edition (Abingdon Press, Nashville, TN, 2003) p. 329. Dr. Metzger reports 5,519 papyri, parchments, and manuscripts of the Bible are now available in 2001.

Chapter 4: The Assault on the OT Canon

*"TAKE THEE ANOTHER ROLL, AND WRITE IN IT **ALL** THE **FORMER WORDS** that were in the first roll which Jehoiakim the king of Judah hath burned."* [Jer. 36:28] God ordered a copy of the original autograph. In other words, God ordered an apograph to be made. This strongly supports and affirms one of the methods of preservation of the inspired words of Scripture.[51] The exact Words were to be copied. No change was to be made in spelling or word order.

God preserved the manuscript prepared by Jeremiah and Baruch by having another one made; a copy of the first manuscript. *"ALL THE WORDS"* were spelled the same and were in the same order. Throughout the OT era, faithful scribes[52] made apographs; accurate copies of the original books of the Bible in Hebrew and Aramaic that contained *"ALL THE WORDS."* Paul indicates that Timothy had access to those copies [2 Tim 3:15]. The Lord Jesus Christ indicated that *"ALL THE WORDS"* were still present and preserved when he walked this earth and spoke the phrase, *"It is written (gregraptai)"* and by using other like Words[53] [cf. Mat 4:4, Mat. 5:17-20, 24:35, Lk. 24:44]. Furthermore, the virtually identical TT/RT manuscripts confirm their preservation. Additionally, preserved ancient translations into the languages of other nations confirm the authenticity of the "Words." Lastly, God commanded translations [Rom. 16:25, 1 Cor. 14:21, Col. 1:5-6]. All of these methods are mechanisms for man to authenticate His Words in spite of the attack upon them.

---

[51] 2 Tim. 3:15 confirms that Timothy had copies or apographs.
[52] Dr. D. A. Waite, Th.D., Ph.D., *Defending the King James Bible* (Bible For Today Press, Collingswood, NJ, 1995) p. 23-26.
[53] Ibid. pp. 9-11. (Waite, *Defending the King James Bible*).

The Attack on the Canon by Indifference, Neglect, and Apostasy

Another example of "the attack" on the OT Canon will be given before moving on to the attack on the New Testament. Young King Josiah ordered the *"house of the Lord"* to be repaired (2 Kg. 22:5). In the process Hilkiah, the high priest at that time, found the neglected and ignored *"book of the law."* Shaphan, the king's scribe, took the long neglected "book," which was lost because of the apostasy of previous administrations, to the young King Josiah. When he heard *"the words of the book,"* he became distraught and rent his clothes. He cried out: *"our fathers have **not** hearkened unto the words of this book, to do according unto all that which is written concerning us."* [2 Kg. 22:13] My prayer, and hopefully yours, is that the young people of today will be able to cry out, "Our fathers HAVE hearkened unto the Words of this book." However, the current testimony is contrary to this prayer as we will see.

God sent a message to the young King Josiah:

> *"THUS SAITH THE LORD, Behold, I will bring evil upon this place, and upon the inhabitants thereof, even **ALL THE WORDS OF THE BOOK** which the king of Judah hath read: Because they have forsaken me, and have burned incense unto other gods, that they might provoke me to anger with all the works of their hands; therefore my wrath shall be kindled against this place, and shall not be quenched." [2 Kings 22:16-17] [My emphasis]*

The Attack on the Canon Answered by Wrath, Sometimes Delayed

The wrath of God was delayed, however, until King Josiah was gathered into the grave in peace. Why? God gave the answer:

> *Because **THINE HEART WAS TENDER**, and thou hast **HUMBLED THYSELF** before the LORD, **WHEN THOU HEARDEST WHAT I SPAKE** against this place, and against the inhabitants thereof, that they should become a desolation and a curse, and hast **RENT THY CLOTHES**, and **WEPT BEFORE ME**; I also have heard thee, saith the LORD. [2 Kings 22:19] [My emphasis]*

Worthy to note in this passage is that:

1. God reported **all** his written Words [v. 16] were intact and still available after years of neglect as shown by the phrase, "thou heardest what I spake," [v. 19] and

2. God demands and expects honor and respect for **all** His Words. God said to the king, *"thine heart was tender, and thou hast humbled thyself before the LORD.... and wept before me."* [v. 19]

3. For God to hear our **prayers**, He demands esteem for His preserved Words that he has magnified above His name [Psa 138:2]. He said to the king, *"Because... when thou heardest what I spake... I ALSO HAVE HEARD THEE."* [v. 19]

Praise God that this author belongs to an organization, the Dean Burgon Society,[54] which honors, respects, guards, and protects what God "spake." However, the prayers of many "great" and "wise" men [scholars] are ***not*** heard because they have ***not*** heard what God

---

[54] www.deanburgonsociety.org.

"spake." Their hearts are not tender; they have not humbled themselves; they have not wept before the LORD. This is the topic of our next section about the NT.

What's more, the Lord Jesus Christ indicated that the Hebrew text, which "He had preserved unto Himself"[55] and which would never disappear (Mat. 5:18, 24:35) was still present and used by Him in Luke 24:44 saying:

> *"And he said unto them, These are the words which I spake unto you, while I was yet with you, that all things must be fulfilled, which were written in the law of Moses, and in the prophets, and in the psalms, concerning me."*

Jesus indicated that the three parts of the Jewish Bible:

> "[t]he law (*torah*), the prophets (*Nebiim*), and the writings, (*ketubim*) ...made up the Hebrew OT and is called the Tanak."[56]

Before proceeding, please keep in mind the following three (3) items:

Remember: 1. The Canon of the Old Testament is Preserved

God has providentially preserved His Words found in the OT books in spite of the horrendous attack upon them. Dr. D. A. Waite, president of the DBS reports:

---

[55] Dr. Thomas Strouse, "Scholarly Myths Perpetuated on Rejecting the Masoretic Text of the OT" (DBS Message Book, Collingswood, NJ, 2003) p. 191. Dr. Strouse's comments on Mat 4:4 are also very apropos and may be found at www.emmanuel-newington.org/seminary/resources/index.php.
[56] Ibid. p. 193.

"Robert Dick Wilson[57] believed the Masoretic Traditional Hebrew Text that existed in Christ's day was in existence from the beginning. "Henry W. Coray, in reflecting on the life and ministry of Robert Dick Wilson, a man who had mastered some '45 ancient languages and dialects' and who 'was a staunch defender of the doctrine of verbal inspiration of Holy Scripture,' affirmed that Wilson accepted as accurate the Masoretic Hebrew Text. Coray, quoting Wilson, wrote: 'The result of those thirty years study [Wilson wrote this]: I can affirm that there is not a page of the Old Testament concerning which we need have any doubt. We can be absolutely certain that substantially we have the text of the Old Testament that Christ and the Apostles had, and which was in existence from the beginning.'"[58]

Remember: 2. God's Warning

The second item to remember before we proceed is God's warning to those who have not yet experienced God's wrath for corrupting His words [Rev. 22:18-19]:

"Because sentence against an evil work IS NOT EXECUTED SPEEDILY, therefore the heart of the sons of men is fully set in them to do evil" [Eccles. 8:11].

Remember: 3. There are False Claims

The third item to remember is that there are many *false* claims that modern archaeological discoveries, such as the manuscripts at Qumran (DSS), have shed "new" light on the inspiration and preservation of the Canon of the Bible. *The Canon Debate* by editors L. M. McDonald and James A. Sanders casts considerable doubt on a closed Old Testament Canon by using scholarolatry, by using their

---

[57] See Appendix for a description of Robert Dick Wilson.
[58] Dr. D. A. Waite, Th.D., Ph.D., *The Case For The KJV* (Bible For Today Press, Collingwood, NJ, BFT #83) pp. 11, 14.

"claims" related to the Essene's manuscripts, and by exalting manuscripts of Samaritan origins. Neither the Samaritans nor the Essenes were charged with preserving the OT Canon, which were the "oracles" of God. The Jews were responsible. That is what the Scripture says [Rom. 3:2].

In addition, evidence from the Nag Hammadi Gnostic archeological site is particularly promoted as evidence to support their contention that the Canon of Scripture was open early and should still be open.[59] Dr. Ehrman implies in his work, *Lost Christianities,* that the books found at the Nag Hammadi site ***possibly*** support other sayings of Jesus left out of the Canon that should be there. Of course, this is not ***possibly*** wrong; it is wrong, as we shall see.

---

[59] Bart Ehrman, *Lost Christianities, The Battles For Scripture and the Faiths We Never Knew* (Oxford University Press, New York, 2003) p. 51. Dr. Ehrman states: "And in the opinion of probably the majority of scholars of early Christianity, these are the most significant manuscript discoveries of modern times."

CHAPTER 5

THE ATTACK ON THE NT CANON

For we are not as many, which corrupt the word of God: but as of sincerity, but as of God, in the sight of God speak we in Christ. 2 Corinthians 2:17

Many Corrupt the Words of God

The New Testament era is plagued with corrupters whose *"heart...is fully set in them to do evil."* [Ecc. 8:11] Paul made it abundantly clear that there were many corrupters of God's words. He said, *"For we are not as **MANY, which corrupt the word of God**"* [2 Cor. 2:17a]. Paul's comment alludes to the Greek paraphrases of the Torah by the dispersed Jews, to the cultic charges and changes in Scripture appearing because of Gnostics, and to the corrupted Samaritan Pentateuch that was available in the first century.

The Septuagint (LXX)

The *Greek translation* of the OT and *revision* (corruption) of the entire NT occurred soon *after* the Lord Jesus Christ's first parousia. The translation and revision became known as the Septuagint. Origen (184-254 A.D.) named one column in his six column work on the OT and NT called the *Hexapla*, the LXX.[60]

---

[60] McDonald, op. cit., p. 72 (*The Canon Debate*). The Septuagint, a Greek paraphrase of the OT, was not named, Septuagint, until

LXX, which stands for seventy, is derived from a fraudulent letter most likely written to support the sale of a Greek OT translation.[61] It mentions seventy priests who allegedly translated the OT from Hebrew into Greek in two weeks. The priests worked separately, but their translations were reported to be miraculously the same. Origen added apocryphal books to his revision of the LXX and the NT (Septuagint). There were also several other Greek translations of the OT by other men available soon after the Apostolic era. Every revision of the Septuagint (LXX) since Origen has contained the Apocrypha. It is sometimes also called the "G" because it is a Greek translation of the OT and a revision of the Greek NT. Alexandria was the city in Egypt where Origen carried out his well-known but infamous work.

The Gnostic and Arian corrupters were at work very early in Alexandria. God said, *"Woe unto them that call evil good, and good evil; that put darkness for light, and light for darkness; that put bitter for sweet, and sweet for bitter!"* [Isa. 5:20]. God calls His Words, light. [Psa 119:105, Prov. 6:23]. In essence, corrupters are changing His Words and calling their words light. Their Words are lying words (cf. Jer. 7:8, 29:23). He often warned anyone who would corrupt His Words [Deut. 4:2, Prov. 30:6, Rev. 22:18-19].

Augustine of Hippo (354-430 A.D.); *The Canon Debate*, p. 72. Rather, it was called the LXX early in the NT era.

[61] H. D. Williams, *The Septuagint is a Paraphrase, The Character of God's Words is Not Found in the LXX or the "G"* (The Old Paths Publications, Cleveland, GA, 2008). The fraudulent letter is the named *The Letter of Aristeas*.

Other Attacks Through the Centuries

Many authors through the centuries report the horrendous attack on the letters, Words, passages, and books of the Bible.[62] Some writers attribute the worst attacks to have occurred during the first two hundred years after the recording of the books of the NT. However long, the attack has been relentless. When Jerome constructed the Latin Vulgate from Alexandrian MSS, the Waldensians, Vigilantius, Jovinian, and Helvidius in Northern Italy chastised him for his version of the Latin Bible. Jerome's reaction was very nasty.[63]

Consider the attacks on the early Christians and their records by the Roman emperors. Thousands of Christians were slaughtered and the emperors burned their Bibles. In the dark ages, the Waldensians, who were known also by many other names, were massacred and their records destroyed by the Roman Catholic Church.

Later on, consider the attack by the notorious Brooke Foss Westcott (1825-1903) and Fenton John Anthony Hort (1828-1893) in the nineteenth century,[64] and for that matter, many of the preceding 17th and 18th century rationalists such as Griesbach, Semler, and Lachmann. Westcott and Hort (19th century) produced the vile "new" Greek text used by essentially all modern common-language translations, such as the NIV, NLB, NASB, ERV, and RSV.

In spite of the attacks, many godly men, who have done extensive research, affirm the preservation of the Scriptures. God's

---

[62] Burgon, Dean John William; *The Revision Revised*, (The Dean Burgon Society Press, Collingswood, NJ) The Dean repeatedly mentions the relentless attacks during the first several centuries.
[63] Williams, op. cit. 235-242 (*The Lie That Changed the Modern World*).
[64] Dr. D. A. Waite, Th.D. Ph.D., *The Heresies of Westcott and Hort* (Bible For Today, Collingswood, NJ.) These men were apostate.

promise to preserve His Words is true. Although a believer needs nothing more than the promises in Scripture, the Words of God are reinforced:
1. by thousands of copies of MSS,
2. by translations into other languages,
3. by lectionaries, and
4. by many quotes from various authors and church elders throughout the centuries.

This has frustrated the modernist and postmodernist scholars because they cannot believe God preserved His words, even with the overwhelming evidence that He did. They continue to spend millions of dollars digging around in caves, garbage dumps, and graves. Perhaps they should spend the money on orphans and widows as commanded.

Contemptuously, the textual critics have thrust on the world their "new" fabricated texts from approximately 45 New Testament corrupt manuscripts and a few corrupt Old Testament manuscripts, while ignoring:
1. what the Scriptures promise,
2. that the preserved Words were in existence from generation to generation, and
3. that the Words are verified in the majority of manuscripts, numbering 5,519 as of 2003.[65]

Since about 1962, because of the naturalistic text critic Kurt Aland, scholars have gone a step farther than rejecting some of the Words preserved from *"generation to generation."* Now they are

---

[65] Bruce M. Metzger, *The New Testament;, Its Background, Growth, and Content* (Abingdon Press, Nashville; 3rd Edition, 2003) p. 329.

clamoring for a "new" canon of Scripture.[66] Many textual critics are asking for the removal of some orthodox canonical books and replacing them with documents that had been rejected by the Bible-believing churches many centuries ago.[67] There are many reports concerning the desire of the Roman Catholic Church to replace the NT book of Revelation. For example:

> "No wonder U.S. News and World Report magazine, in its 11-8-93 issue reveals plans by Canon Seminar scholars for a "radical revision of the New Testament" that will replace the Book of Revelation with "Other writings ...[previously] dismissed by church leaders as unauthentic or heretical."[68]

How many other books, including OT books, will be replaced if the door is opened to scholars?

Canon Criticism

This presentation hopes to illuminate or shine a light upon the current attack on the Canon of Scripture. The natural progression of textual criticism has been from denying the preservation of "jots and tittles" (letters) to rejecting the books of the Bible. The 'new' discipline of *Canon Criticism* is only amplifying the problem. It is hoped that in this brief work some illumination can be focused on what the modernistic 'scholars' assert in regard to the Canon of Scripture. Their assertions are that the COS:

---

[66] Lee Martin McDonald and James Sanders, Editors, *The Canon Debate* (Hendrickson Publishers, Peabody, Massachusetts 2002). This is the import of this entire book.
[67] Ibid. 288 (*The Canon Debate*).
[68] George Theiss, "Which Bible?" (www.tulipgems.com/WhichBible2.htm).

1. is a sham,
2. is related to Gnosticism, and
3. is harming our children.

Their claim that the COS is harming our children is moot. They are inappropriately implying that Christian values and beliefs are too legalist and rigid. Many claim that children raised in Christian homes are very innocent and poorly prepared for the world and its values. This is false. When students study the traditional COS, their performance and preparation excels according to universities and colleges. Even their employers, such as lawyers, doctors, and schools, pour out accolades. Their average test scores on national exams are better. Their success in life is so far ahead of secular trained students that there is no comparison.

Their claim that Christianity is linked to Gnosticism is just as fallacious. Their reasoning goes along the following lines and is related to the desire of many current scholars to introduce heretical Gnostic books into the Canon. Why? Sadly, modern day scholars place ***early*** heretics, such as the Gnostics, **and** orthodox sanctified believers into one faction called *"proto-Christians."* They assert that heretics like the Gnostics deserve the right to be called Christians because they believed in Jesus Christ even if they believed unorthodox ideas.[69] In addition, many scholars assert Christian beliefs to be mystical, just like some of the early Gnostics.

---

[69] Ehrman, op. cit., pp. 1, 256 (*Lost Christianities*). This thought totally disregards Paul's warnings about "another gospel," [Gal. 1:6-9] and is evidence of neo-evangelicals' subtle permission for "scholars" to be even bolder. Dr. Ehrman's basic theme is "the need for tolerance"; in light of his belief that the canon of Scripture, the Words of God, or the Bible is not resolved. He believes the Bible was constructed from many forged documents for the "proto-orthodox" to win the battle for dominance.

Their implication is that the early schismatics and heretics were not as bad as they have been characterized by previous generations and by some modern writers, including this author. They assert that we must be more "tolerant."[70] This is reminiscent of the neo-evangelical call by Harold Ockenga in 1948 to "tolerance." His call included a *"ringing call to repudiation of separatism."*[71] There is an old saying, "Birds of a feather, flock together." Does the Bible call for separation from those who would corrupt the Bible? Of course, it does and in many places (cf. Rom. 16:17-18, 2 Thes. 3:6, 14, 2 Jn 10-11). Many verses in the NT warn of the struggles by the "orthodox" (Acts 20:29, Jude 4).

Scholars Claim Fraudulent Books Are in the Sacred Canon

Many present-day modernists and postmodernists assert that recent scholarship and archaeological discoveries prove an early power struggle *within* the church for dominance that was won by "proto-orthodox" Christians. They allege the "proto-orthodox" authorities successfully silenced the other "proto-Christian" groups competing for dominance in the first several centuries. The modernists **surmise** that Christianity could have gone in many other directions if some other group had won the power struggle. Groups such as the Ebionites, Marcosians, Adoptionists, Subordinists, Docetists, Dualists, Carpocratians, Marcionites, Montanists, Theodotians, Valentinians, and others could have won the upper hand. However, the scholars

---

[70] Ibid. p. 256.
[71] Cloud, Dr. David, "Biblical Inspiration, Part I," (Way of Life Literature, Port Huron, MI, June 14, 2004) p. 4-5.

assert these groups were suppressed due to politics, intrigue, forgeries, and deceit by the "proto-orthodox."

The guidance of the Holy Spirit and the immediate recognition of canonical works by the early sanctified churches are never considered or mentioned by modern Gnostic scholars claiming superior knowledge. They cannot understand God's providential hand at work (Rom 11:33, 1 Cor. 1:19).

Nevertheless, their claim is that the early battles had nothing to do with *correct* doctrine, but with *power* struggles *within* the church for dominance.[72] This has the same ring to it as the assertions of *critical text* proponents and their genealogical (family) arguments such as Westcott and Hort's arguments. They claim that powerful church revisionists suppressed the "real" original text. Their claims are repeatedly shown to be false.[73] The *"proto-orthodox"* 'family' theory is also false. Early Christianity was not a family struggle. The early *"orthodox Christians"* were butchered mercilessly.

Many scholars go much further than the family theory, however, and claim that this struggle produced pseudonymous, fraudulent works that have found their way into the Bible as part of the Canon of Scripture.

---

[72] Ehrman; op. cit.; p. 2 (*Lost Christianities*). He claims early "Christians" believed many unorthodox beliefs. He cannot maintain this unusual claim without redefining the term "Christian," which he clearly does not accomplish.

[73] Dr. H. D Williams, M. D. Ph.D., *The Lie That Changed The Modern World, A Refutation of the Modernist Cry: "Poly-Scripturae,"* (Bible For Today Press; Collingswood, NJ, 2004) p. 191-196.

Chapter 5: The Assault on the NT Canon

More False Claims

For example, in his books, *Lost Christianities, Misquoting Jesus, Lost Scriptures,* and *The New Testament, An Historical Introduction To The Early Christian Writings,* Dr. Bart Ehrman repeatedly verifies his belief that canonical books are forged.[74] Many of his students and others will read his books because he is Chairman of the Department of Religious Studies at the University of North Carolina at Chapel Hill. Dr. Ehrman states:

> As we will see, these confrontations were waged largely on literary grounds, as members of the proto-orthodox group produced polemical tractates in opposition to other Christian perspectives, FORGED SACRED TEXTS to provide authorization for their own perspectives (FORGERIES, THAT IS, CLAIMING TO BE WRITTEN BY JESUS OWN APOSTLES), AND COLLECTED OTHER EARLY WRITINGS INTO A SACRED CANON OF SCRIPTURE TO ADVANCE <u>THEIR VIEWS</u> and counteract the views of others. It is out of these conflicts that the New Testament came into being, a collection of twenty-seven books TAKEN TO BE SACRED, INSPIRED, and AUTHORITATIVE.[75] [My emphasis, but **not** my addition in parentheses, which is Dr. Ehrman's statement.]

---

[74] Dr. Robert J. Barnett, "Turretin," (DBS Message Book, Collingwood, NJ, 1991). "Turretin said, 'Most papists contend that many canonical books have been lost in order that thus they may prove the imperfection of Scripture and the necessity of tradition to supply its defects.'"

[75] Ibid. p. 7. Dr. Ehrman continues by supplying his readers with a list of forged canonical books in the remainder of his book that can only be characterized by Paul's statement in Gal. 1:8, "let him be accursed." His theories cannot be proven and only serve to confuse many.

Claims of False Books

Dr. Ehrman maintains that 2 Thessalonians, Colossians, Ephesians, 1 and 2 Timothy, Titus, Jude, Hebrews, 1 and 2 Peter, Revelation, and the synoptic gospels are frauds.[76]

Dr. Ehrman says that modern forms of so-called Christianity emerged from one dominant Christian group that overpowered the many so-called "Christianities" of the early era. He says,

> "But virtually all forms of modern Christianity, whether they acknowledge it or not, go back to **one form** of Christianity that emerged as victorious from the conflicts [of many "Christianities"] of the second and third centuries.[77] [my addition and emphasis, HDW]

The "one form" Dr. Ehrman speaks about is the scholar's "proto-Christian" group.

In other words, Dr. Ehrman, a teacher of college students, our children, has completely belittled the verbal, plenary, inspired, preserved Canon of Scripture and the priesthood of believers who have guarded, protected, and preserved God's Words by their very lives.[78] The registrar at the University of North Carolina reports the average number of students that graduate per year from UNC at Chapel Hill is 6,579.[79] Each student is required to take a philosophy or religion course. Dr. Ehrman has been at UNC for over ten (10) years. You do the math.

---

[76] Ibid. p. 235, 242, 243.
[77] Ibid. p. 4. The correct information is that there has been two "routes," (Mat. 7:13-14) since the Garden. One route was the Bible-believing or God fearing route. The second route is a broad way that leads to destruction.
[78] J. van Braght Thieleman, *Martyrs Mirror* (Herald Press, Scottdale, PA; 1950) pp. 5-60.
[79] This number is the average during the years preceding 2005.

Chapter 5: The Assault on the NT Canon

Dr. Ehrman and his colleagues assertion is that anyone who mentioned the name of the Lord Jesus Christ in the first two centuries was a "proto-orthodox" Christian, even if they believed in scholasticism (Greek philosophy and Scripture mixed) and Gnosticism.

False Claims Refuted

Harold O. J. Brown, a graduate of Harvard University, anticipated the approach that would be taken by modern and postmodern scholars. In his book, *Heresies*, he reports on the foolishness of the idea that splinter groups attempted to hijack Christianity. Writing in 1988, Dr. Brown said:

> "until recently IT WAS THOUGHT THAT THE WHOLE MOVEMENT (Gnosticism) WAS A PHENOMENON WITHIN THE CHURCH."[80] "The Gnostic movement as a whole and even church-related Gnosticism are really too big and too foreign to the New Testament to be called heresies; **THEY REALLY REPRESENT AN ALTERNATIVE RELIGION.**"[81] [My emphasis]

Apparently, Dr. Ehrman does not understand or does not get the message that Dr. Brown presents or that the Bible presents [Gal. 1]. Dr. Ehrman considers Gnosticism part of early "Christianities." Dr. Ehrman is another author who is chipping away at the very foundations by making theoretical claims in his writings; claims which are suppositions characterized by the words "perhaps," "maybe," "could be," etc. Claims cannot be used to establish truth. He apparently does not understand or believe most of the NT writings. He uses suppositions to pronounce most of Paul's letters as fraudulent works.

---

[80] Harold O. J. Brown, Ph.D., *Heresies* (Hendrickson Publishers, Peabody, Massachusetts, 1988) p. 44.
[81] Ibid. p. 52.

The Attack on the Canon of Scripture

This is dangerous ground. Why? See Chapter 8. This author believes God preserved His words in a Canon of Scripture as He said He would. [Psa. 12:6-7, Mat. 4:4, 5:17-18, 1 Pe. 1:23-25, etc.]

Paul warned about:

1. fables [1 Tim 1:4],
2. old wives tales [1 Tim 4:7],
3. blasphemers [2 Tim 3:2],
4. speaking lies in hypocrisy [1 Tim. 4:1-2a],
5. perverse disputings of men of corrupt minds, destitute of and resisting the truth [1 Tim 6:5, 2 Tim 3:8],
6. profane and vain babblings [2 Tim 2:16], and
7. their "science falsely so-called" [1 Tim. 6:20],
8. their words would eat as a canker, overthrowing the ignorant in unbelief [2 Tim 2:17, 18], which we will demonstrate have produced *"**a** curse"* on the earth [Mal. 4:6],
9. those *"overthrown,"* who would heap to themselves teachers after their own lusts since they have *"itching ears"* [2 Tim 4:3],
10. being aware *"of unruly and vain talkers"* [Titus 1:10-11] *"teaching things they ought not"* [Titus 1:11],
11. not teaching the *"wholesome words"* of Christ [1 Tim 6:3], and to rightly divide the Words of truth, which is the Canon of Scripture [2 Tim. 2:15] and if they do not, the folly of those who do not speak THE TRUTH will be manifest to all men. [2 Tim 3:9].

He also said their *"mouths must be stopped"* [Titus 1:11] and ***"to rebuke them sharply"*** [Titus 1:13].

This is the intent of this work. In addition, it is to show that many of the modern and postmodern scholars fit Paul's description and that they fall into the trap of Gnosticism's great promise of salvation through knowledge; whether universally applied to all men or whether applied to an individual's salvation. They profess knowledge, evolution, and *"science, falsely so-called"* as the route to a better life and the answers to all the mysteries of the universe. They need to be rebuked *"sharply."* They 'smell' like Gnostics.

CHAPTER 6

WHO WERE THE GNOSTICS?

"For if a man think himself to be something, when he is nothing, he deceiveth himself" Galatians 6:3.

The Gnostics were **not** part of the orthodox Bible-believing assemblies.[82] They had their own "churches," but they were *not identified* with Bible-believing churches.[83] They had their own monasteries such as the monastery at Nag Hammadi (Chenoboskion).[84]

A similar phenomenon today is found in the New Age assemblies, Unitarian assemblies, postmodern "communities," Wiccan organizations, certain "charismatic" universities and schools, Mormon churches, Seventh-day Adventist churches, and organized atheist groups. They are religious. They have a form of religion and of godliness, but without power (2 Tim 3:1-5). There have been numerous doctrinally unsound organizations throughout history and as expected from Scripture, there have been few Bible-believing churches (Mat. 7:14, Lk. 8:18, Rev. 3). Nevertheless, consider the influence COS-believing churches have had.

---

[82] Ibid. p. 95.
[83] Green, op. cit., p. 412. (*Unholy Hands on the* Bible; Vol. II). Marcion was kicked out of the church at Rome and started his own churches called Marcionite churches, and many persisted into the 5th century. This is similar to Mormon churches, Kingdom Halls, Roman Catholic parishes, etc.
[84] Metzger, op. cit., p. 118. (*The New Testament, its Background, Growth, and Content*). More than 40 works, mostly Gnostic, were found in a jar there. Chenoboskion, an ancient Gnostic library.

The early Gnostic movement or philosophy can also be compared to elements within modern-day mysticism, transcendentalism, existentialism, and the religion of evolution.[85] These philosophical movements are outside **Bible-believing** churches, but they are influencing them.

The Gnostic movement certainly caused the early "orthodox" Bible-believing churches to define clearly certain doctrines FROM THE SCRIPTURES,[86] but there is absolutely no proof that Bible-believers forged "tractates," or letters, or books that *became* part of the Canon of the Bible. There is also no evidence of murder, subterfuge, or deceit by sanctified churches. Dr. Brown said:

> "If early Christian theology represented a Hellenization of theology in the effort to resist Gnosticism, then it would be necessary to say that although Gnosticism could not conquer Christianity, it forced it to destroy itself. If, however, early Christian theology represents a legitimate and necessary working out, in Hellenistic terms, of the authentic Gospel, then Gnosticism actually performed a service for the church, by compelling it to think the Gospel through and work out it implications."[87]

1. Gnostics Often "Went Out From" Bible-believing Churches

There were schools in existence very early that taught scholasticism, Arianism, legalism, and other perverted doctrine. There is considerable evidence that heretical groups and apostate individuals

---

[85] Ibid. p. 44.
[86] Brown, op. cit., p. 41 (*Heresies*).
[87] Ibid. 41. (*Heresies*) (This is Adolf von Harnack's idea as reported in *Heresies*).

Chapter 6: Who Were the Gnostics?

changed the Scriptures, such as Origen,[88] who was an Arian. Another is Marcion, who hated Jews and cut out references to Israel from the Gospels. The Gnostics, such as Marcion (ca. 110-160 A.D.), were kicked out of the churches. The "orthodox" immersed believers **guarded**, **protected**, and **kept** the Words of God as commanded (Jn. 14:`5, 23 and many places). There is no other explanation for the great number of virtually identical manuscripts from widely separated geographical regions. Certainly, unorthodox believers were disciplined and removed from doctrinally sound churches. Some apostates even *"went out from"* or left the orthodox churches and taught false doctrines. The NT calls our attention to these apostates (Acts 15:24, 1 Jn. 2:19). Albert Barnes comments on 1 Jn 2:19. He said:

> "Verse 19. *They went out from us.* From the church. That is, they had once been professors of the religion of the Saviour, though their apostasy showed that they never had any true piety. John refers to the fact that they had once been in the church, perhaps to remind those to whom he wrote that they knew them well, and could readily appreciate their character. It was a humiliating statement that those who showed themselves to be so utterly opposed to religion had once been members of the Christian church; but this is a statement which we are often compelled to make."

Obviously, there were sanctified churches from the beginning with immersed believers who were following doctrine derived from the *"foundation of the Apostles and prophets;"* Words received from God that became the COS (Eph. 2:20). Individuals left the sanctified churches to start their own "denominations." God did not bless those

---

[88] James H. Sightler, M. D., *A Testimony Founded For Ever* (Sightler Publications, Greenville, SC; 2nd Edition, 2001) p. 54. Sightler says: "Origen, [who] was probably the worst heretic and perverter of scripture in history."

heretical and apostate groups; so, they failed. Therefore, Bible-believing churches today are "compelled to make" corrections to views by scholars that cannot be sustained. There is only SPECULATION from *unbelievers* about "proto-Christianities" and "proto-orthodox" groups who love terms such as:

1. "perhaps,"
2. "if,"
3. "maybe,"
4. "might have been,"
5. "could be,"
6. "evidently,"
7. "may have,"
8. "is it because,"
9. "could they have been?,"
10. "suggesting that,"
11. "appears to go back,"
12. "widely held suspicion,"
13. "if this view is right," and many more speculative terms.[89]

There were sound churches from the beginning. Most apostate and heretical groups have tried to crush, eliminate, hush, kill, obliterate records, destroy individuals, and perform other sordid atrocities to the "orthodox" saints through the centuries. The "orthodox" have always been in the minority. Certainly, there is evidence that the emerging state-church of Constantine, which became the Roman Catholic Church, murdered, persecuted, corrupted,

---

[89] A very responsible teenager in our church took Bart Ehrman's *Lost Christianities*, and counted the number of occurrences of these type terms, which indicate speculation. The total was 371 occurrences. See Appendix 10.

destroyed, and forged documents. Even those measures could not destroy the providential care of God's COS-believing churches. Furthermore, the state-church, which merged Babylonian beliefs with Christian doctrine, cannot be lumped with the early Bible-believing churches such as those of the Novatians, the Donatists, the Waldensians, the Albigensians, the Lollards, or whatever name is applied to those churches filled with the priesthood of believers.[90] The speculative reasoning of the modernists:

> "is all argumentum ad hominem reasoning. This type of argument is built on a series of surmises. Those who use these kinds of arguments forget the difference between conclusions based on facts compared to a conclusion based on theory, probability, and/or presumption. The strongest conclusions based on these types of arguments can never rise above a probability. But to promote the conclusion as truth, which is **not based** on prima facie evidence known to the persons or individuals, BECOMES A LIE.[91]

The early Bible-believing churches not only identified forgeries and heretical books, but they also warned others about them. Some copies of these false productions survived because they were not used much or they were buried with their deceased adherents. One such find is the Gnostic writings found buried in a grave at Nag Hammadi. An example of a warning about those "heretical" books that was given to the churches is Athanasius' (296-373 A.D.) admonition:

---

[90] This author realizes there have been some individuals among orthodox Bible believing churches who have become schismatic or apostate, but it is wrong to label an entire group as heretical, such as the Novatians and others who have often been falsely accused.
[91] H. D. Williams, M.D., *The Lie That Changed The Modern World* (Bible For Today Press, Collingswood, NJ, 2004) p. 30-31.

> "It was the year 367...that the powerful bishop of Alexandria, Athanasius, wrote a letter to the churches throughout Egypt under his jurisdiction, in which he laid out in strict terms the contours of the canon of Scripture....Moreover, Athanasius insisted that other "heretical" books not be read."[92]

Some documents were forged for sinister reasons to promote an agenda,[93] but they were identified and removed by Bible-believing churches. Other early documents were written as polemics and were much respected.[94] Sometimes manuscripts were even initially thought to be Scripture by some churches, such as the *Gospel of Peter* and the *Shepherd of Hermas*.[95] However, Bible believing churches under the guidance of the Holy Spirit determined that these influential books were not part of the inspired canon.[96] How? The Holy Spirit guided them *"into all truth."*

The modern scholar seems to have little regard for the recognition of the Canon of Scripture by the Holy Spirit's guidance[97] [2 Pe 1:21] and for its immediate acceptance as Scripture by the early orthodox believers [2 Pe 3:15-16]. Of course, if you have not experienced salvation (*"born again"*) and therefore, have not become a *"new creature,"* understanding the work of the Holy Spirit will be dim [2 Cor. 5:17, John 3:3, Job 19: 23-27, 32:8-9]. The work of the Holy

---

[92] Ehrman, op. cit. pp. 54, 230-231 (*Lost Christianities*). Ehrman speculates that the reason the Nag Hammadi jars containing Gnostic books were found was because there was an attempt to hide the manuscripts from Athanasius.
[93] Ibid. p. 81-89.
[94] F. F. Bruce, *The Canon of Scripture* (Intervarsity Press, Downer's Grove, IL, 1988) pp. 200-203. Also, see Ehrman, op. cit., p. 121 (*Lost Christianities*).
[95] Ibid. p. 200.
[96] Tertullian's eventual identification of the *Shepherd of Hermas* as a book that does not belong in the canon is an example.
[97] Strouse, op. cit. p. 71 (*The Lord Hath Spoken*).

Spirit is not knowable through the five senses. That would be a Montanus' type view. Contrary to Scripture, Montanus believed that the Holy Spirit gave him and his two female disciples, Maximilla and Prisca, special prophetic (foretelling) gifts and that the Holy Spirit spoke audibly and directly to him.[98] When a believer speaks about the guidance of the Holy Spirit, he means the illumination or enlightenment of the precise Words of Scripture (Jn. 1:9, Eph. 1:18, 3:9). The Spirit shines a light on the Words to enhance a believers understanding. Gnostics seem to claim extra-Biblical special knowledge received through the senses. It is often mystical and it cannot be verified. The Lord Jesus Christ's life (including miracles), his confirmation of the OT COS, death, burial, and resurrection provide undeniable evidence of the Christian faith as recorded in the COS.

Of course, if you do not believe and have not accepted the Truth in the COS, one way to get rid of the proofs that would stand-up in a court of law and that are so mysterious to many people, is to declare them **"forgeries."**[99] With that one word, supported by theories, guesses, possibilities, or suppositions, a scholar can destroy the innocent. Isn't this what the *Canon Debate* is all about?

2. Gnostics and Scholars Are Similar

Those with a "low" view of Scripture and of the work of the Holy Spirit in the churches, have common characteristics, which lead to denigration of the Scripture. They are:

---

[98] Brown, *Heresies,* p. 66ff.
[99] Ehrman, *Lost Christianities,* p. 235.

1. Denial:[100] (For example, the *denial* of the 330 fulfilled prophecies located in many canonical books concerning the Lord Jesus Christ. The fulfillment of these prophecies has great theological and apologetic significance. Also, consider the *denied* prophecies concerning (1.) Cyrus, (2.) the Babylonian 70 year captivity, (3.) the four hundred (400) year Egyptian sojourn.)
2. Inference:[101] They *attribute* the meaning of facts to their view, exclusively, and without regard to other possibilities.
3. Supposition: They guess at the motives of writers *unknown to them*; especially pseudonymous authors of spurious books. No one may even know who wrote a book about which many scholars make special claims of knowledge .
4. Evolutionary beliefs: Everything evolves—creation, doctrines, churches, society (out of conflicts), books of the Bible (conflation), language, linguistic abilities, religion, ideas, aeons, etc. This is a polemical position that cannot be sustained by evidence.[102]

---

[100] Sanders, op. cit., ("The Family in the Bible," Biblical Theology Bulletin, Fall, 2002). Sanders, Clermont School of Theology, says, "Emmanuel = God with us had always meant God's being with the Jewish people as a whole. Early Christians, however, resignified it and applied it to **their belief** in God's being in one Jew, Christ. Hellenistic individualism permitted them to hear the message that God had resurrected that one person...The concept of Christ being a personal savior is only **marginally** biblical" [WOW!, my emphasis, HDW].
[101] Ehrman, op. cit., p. 141(*Lost Christianities)* and in many places in this book.
[102] Brown, *Heresies*, p. 38.

5. Theory: Theories and assumptions, reported over and over, become facts.[103]
6. Incomplete Facts: These may be either intentional or unintentional.[104]

Their own writings demonstrate each of these failures. These characteristics are not unusual for non-believers. The heretics of the early centuries as well as the heretics of the modern era demonstrate the same tendencies.

3. Gnostic Beliefs

Next, let us examine some of the early heretical beliefs. Why were their beliefs rejected by the "orthodox?" Gnosticism contains broad categories of erroneous beliefs. Nevertheless, their BELIEFS can be filtered into four basic ideas.

1. Dualism: Dualism is the belief that the fundamental nature of existence is the ultimate battle between spirit and matter. The opposite is monism, one authoritative God.[105]
2. Docetism:[106] Docetism is the result of dualism. Gnostics could not believe that Jesus Christ was man since they believed that matter was evil. They argued that our Lord Jesus Christ only "seemed" to be human.

---

[103] Jack P. Lewis, Editors, McDonald and Sanders, *The Canon Debate*; (Hendrickson Publishers, 2002) p. 147-148. The Jamnia hypothesis became fact.
[104] Metzger, op cit., pp. 99-100. The Q source becomes "fact" even without MS support.
[105] Ehrman, op. cit.; p. 119.
[106] Brown, op. cit., pp. 52ff (*Heresies*).

3. Knowledge: Knowledge leads to salvation.[107] This is a belief that the attainment of superior knowledge leads to salvation. This is a works salvation, similar to Lordship salvation, which requires making God Lord of every aspect of your life before you can be saved.
4. Evolution: An elaborate "evolution" of "pleroma" or spirit beings who created and developed the material world. This is an obvious rejection of the Biblical account of creation.[108] The Gnostic beliefs are the early seed of the modern theory of evolution. The **theory** of evolution is also a "religion" that permeates all levels of postmodern society.

4. Attractions to Gnosticism

Two ATTRACTIONS to early Gnosticism persist in modern Gnosticism. These attractions include:
1. The quest for secret lore or wisdom that explains otherwise incomprehensible mysteries and
2. The assertion that its secrets are accessible only to the elite.[109]

5. Tendencies of Gnosticism

Through the centuries, there are three weaknesses and tendencies in the religion of Gnostics. They prove attractive to individuals with unorthodox theological beliefs and to doctrinally weak orthodox individuals. They are:
1   A speculative, philosophical mood (uncertainty),

---

[107] Ibid. p. 39ff.
[108] Sightler, op. cit., pp. 53-54 (*A Testimony Founded For Ever, The King James Bible Defended in Faith and History*).
[109] Brown, op. cit., p. 44 (*Heresies*).

2 Charismatic tendencies, and

3 Asceticism[110]

Many alleged "scholars" in the departments of religion around the world are attracted to numbers one and three. Number two attracts the doctrinally weak. The seed of postmodernism, which is extreme selfism, is detectable in these three items.[111] These three tendencies cannot survive in fundamental Christianity based upon the absolute Truth of the Scriptures. Philosophical uncertainty about any truth, which is prevalent in postmodernism, allows these inclinations and tendencies to be accepted today. The postmodern "communities" (the name for the postmodern church) obviously contain individuals with these attitudes and beliefs.

6. Gnostics and Scholars Compared

The modern scholar's ATTRACTION to certain schools is the claim that only the "initiated" at certain institutions of higher learning can comprehend the facts. Only the "initiated" scholars can "connect the dots" of speculation and facts to arrive at the correct conclusions. The recent attack on the Canon of Scripture is related to the 'secret' or superior knowledge and understanding by individuals trained at Gnostic institutions.[112] Contrary to their claims of "tolerance," the men in charge at these institutions have no tolerance for anyone who believes the literal interpretation of Scripture. Many excellent teachers who are Biblicists are fired when their beliefs become known and do not conform to the majority. For example, many institutions

---

[110] Ibid. p.55.
[111] H. D. Williams, *Hearing the Voice of God* (The Old Paths Publications, Cleveland, GA, 2008) see Chapter 8 particularly.
[112] Ehrman, op. cit., p. 3ff (*Lost Christianities*). Also, James A. Sanders' op. cit., (*The Family and the Bible*).

summarily dismiss professors, who believe creationism. What happened to tolerance?

7. The Apostate School With a Significant Influence

The origin of a modern watershed of apostasy can be identified at the Tubingen school established by F. C. Baur (1792-1860) in Germany. The influence of this school continued in the writings of Walter Bauer (1877-1960), although Walter Bauer is not a founder of the school and is often confused with F. C. Baur.[113] The school is the modern seat of dialectical teaching of religion, which is a spin-off of dialectical materialism.[114] In other words, doctrines, established by systematic examination of the COS, are challenged by humanistic arguments.

The graduates of the school view the wars, conflicts, and vulgarities of history as a human conflict of religious beliefs. As regards the Scriptures, they claim men who professed alleged special revelation constructed self-serving beliefs. Their beliefs contained supernatural imaginative elements designed to achieve group dominance. The bottom line is that they believe the Scriptures were fabricated to support a position of authority. Does this sound like many of the professors at schools around the world today?

---

[113] Brown; op. cit., p. 38 (*Heresies*) and Ehrman, op. cit., pp. 172-176 (*Lost Christianities*).
[114] Dialectical materialism is the "socio-economic theory introduced by Karl Marx (1818-1883) and Friedrich Engels (1820-1895), according to which history and forms of society are interpreted as the result of conflicts between social classes arising from their relations to the means of production." Webster's Dictionary, 1992, J. G. Ferguson Publishing Company, Chicago, IL.

Chapter 6: Who Were the Gnostics?

The German school caused their students to turn to realism, rationalism, alleged tolerance for religious diversity, and intolerance for "orthodox doctrine" established by "authorities." Dr. Ehrman praised F. C. Baur. He said:

> "Baur was a towering figure in the history of nineteenth-century biblical and theological scholarship."[115]

In this author's opinion, the thesis of Bart Ehrman's *Lost Christianities* relates to his belief that the concepts taught at the Tubingen school are more appropriate today than Biblical doctrine. Ehrman believes Scriptures and creeds are useful to:

> "stimulate thought and reflection; they guide action and influence behavior; they provide hope and comfort. And yet many Christians people today are less inclined than their **proto-orthodox** forebears to condemn those who disagree with these teaching. For good or ill, there is a greater sense—though obviously not a universal sense—of **the need for tolerance**."[116]

I could not find any reference in Dr. Ehrman's book about:

> *"So then faith cometh by hearing, and hearing by the word of God" Romans" 10:17. "But without faith it is impossible to please him: for he that cometh to God must believe that he is, and that he is a rewarder of them that diligently seek him" Hebrews 11:6. "That if thou shalt confess with thy mouth the Lord Jesus, and shalt believe in thine heart that God hath raised him from the dead, thou shalt be saved" Romans 10:9. "Well; because of unbelief they were broken off, and thou standest by faith. Be not highminded, but fear: For if God spared not the natural branches, take heed lest he also spare not thee". Romans 11:20-21.*

---

[115] Ehrman, op. cit., 170 (*Lost Christianities*).
[116] Ibid. 256 (*Lost Christianities*).

The speculative philosophical TENDENCY of Gnostics mentioned above is seen in modern and postmodern rationalism. The German Tubingen School is a significant contributor to the spread of humanistic rationalism that spawned or encouraged many modern "isms" such as evolutionism, rationalism, atheism, antisupernaturalism, etc.

> "Although Baur[117] began teaching at Tubingen in 1826, the school's founding is properly dated from the appearance of his pupil D F Strauss's Life of Jesus in 1835. This marked the formal break between the old conservative school and the new radical **antisupernaturalism**. Bauer [sic] himself viewed Jesus in Hegelian[118] terms as the exemplary embodiment of an idea that had greater universal significance than the concrete person of Jesus himself."[119]

The modern scholar's undeniable BELIEF is that science (knowledge) will lead to salvation for humankind on this celestial body, earth. In other words, the preceding means that the superior knowledge of rationalism, technology, and science will lead to

---

[117] One should be aware of Dr. Ehrman's praise of F. C. Baur in *Lost Christianities*; p. 170-172.

[118] Hegelianism is the understanding that "the rational is the real." Obviously, faith is therefore false. "The Hegelian system, in which German Idealism reached its fulfillment, claimed to provide a unitary solution to all of the problems of philosophy. It held that the speculative point of view, which transcends all particular and separate perspectives, must grasp the *one* truth, bringing back to its proper centre all of the problems of logic, of metaphysics (or the nature of Being), and of the philosophies of nature, law, history, and culture (artistic, religious, and philosophical). According to Hegel, this attitude is more than a formal method that remains extraneous to its own content; rather, it represents the actual development of the Absolute—of the all-embracing totality of reality—considered "as Subject and not merely as Substance" (*i.e.*, as a conscious agent or Spirit and not merely as a real being)."
www.kat.gr/kat/history/Mod/Th/Hegelianism.htm.

[119] *Tubingen School,* http://mb-soft.com/believe/txc/tubingen.htm.

universal improvement and salvation for the human race. This is the seed of modern Gnosticism—superior knowledge by humanistic education. If one adds a little mysticism and mystery into the mixture, the result is classic Gnosticism. Rationalism is also the present status of particle or quantum physics and the search for the unifying principle of the universe.[120]

The Gnostic themes listed above lead many scholars, particularly those of a speculative philosophical disposition, to ridiculous conclusions. This author believes that this is a primary reason for seeing the terms, "if," "perhaps," "possible," etc., in their writings. Their agnosticism causes them to discard any aspect or doctrine of the Scriptures. They:

1. Reject Judaism, one God, and the OT,
2. Reject the Logos of the Bible, the unifying factor, in favor of the nebulous logos of Platonism,[121]
3. Reject the God-man of the Bible and believe in the "adoption" of Jesus as a mediator between the cosmos, with its pleroma of created beings, and the "material" world. Many "scholars" believe He was simply a misguided good man, a prophet, a morally influential man, or the prime example of the union of God with all men.

---

[120] The Lord Jesus Christ is the unifying principle. The search for some physical formula that will tie all of the facts related to creation, life and its sustenance together is ridiculous. (cf. Heb. 1:3, Col. 1:15). There is nothing wrong with an investigative mind if the purpose is to honor God and how He accomplished such awesome and miraculous things.
[121] Ulrich, Eugene, in *The Canon Debate*, the chapter on "The Notion and Definition of Canon," calls on scholars to agree with Plato in order to search for a definition of canon. See pages 21 and 35. I ask Dr. Ulrich, "Why not be original and call on the orthodox Canon of Scripture rather than Plato or Socrates?" Additionally, the answers to the simplest to the most complex questions are not found in history but in God's revelation to man.

4. Reject Christianity and believe humanism,[122] scholasticism,[123] or a type of (German) idealism.[124]
5. Reject miracles and providential intervention by God,
6. Reject creation,
7. Reject the virgin birth, and
8. Reject the resurrection of the Lord Jesus Christ.

8. Examples of Modern Gnostics

Gnosticism can be easily identified using three examples:
1. The modern counterpart to the ancient Gnostic's imagination would be the recent television series, *Cosmos,* composed by Carl Sagan. He could allegedly "connect the dots" in evolutionary theory by uniting speculative ideas. Recently, an announcement was made that this series will run again on television.
2. Similarly, some authorities believe that Gnosticism won at least a partial victory by its influence on the tenets of Roman Catholicism and her scholars.[125] Consider their acceptance of purgatory, Mariolatry, transubstantiation, penance, etc. The Babylonian

---

[122] Humanism is defined in the Humanist Manifesto at www.americanhumanist.org/3/HumandItsAspirations.htm.
[123] Scholasticism and Neo-scholasticism are discussed at www.newadvent.org/cathen/10746a.htm and www.newadvent.org/cathen/13548a.htm.
[124] The idealism referred to here is addressed at these sites: www.iep.utm.edu/g/germidea.htm or www.newadvent.org/cathen/07634a.htm or www.seanet.com/~realistic/idealism.html
[125] Ibid. p. 46.

mystery religion that influenced the formation of the Roman Catholic Church is a type of Gnosticism.

3. Lastly, the religion of evolution is a type of Gnosticism at its worst. Scholars who believe evolution will deny this assertion, however. They refuse to believe that their religion is akin to Gnostic speculative philosophical "tendencies." They deny evolution is a humanistic attempt to escape the authority of God. They believe, just like the ancient Gnostics, that their speculations are truth. The real truth is that evolution has no evidence to support it, whereas evidence for biblical truth is exponentially greater. History and archeology continue to reveal just how true the Bible is. Evolutionary Gnosticism is certainly not the *"pure religion"* of the *"Father"* revealed by the Lord Jesus Christ. [Jn. 6:46, Jn 14:9, Jam. 1:27, 1 Jn. 1:2]

9. Where Did Gnosticism Start?

Some early brokers of Gnosticism during the first half of the second century were the Syrian, Saturnilus, or Saturninus, Basilides, the Egyptian, Valentinus, the Roman, and Marcion, the son of a bishop of Sinope.[126]

---

[126] He was born in Sinope, Asia Minor in about 70 A.D.. Marcion was a wealthy merchant and ship owner. After being accused of "defiling a virgin" and reportedly excommunicated by the church in Sinope, Marcion left Asia Minor and moved to Rome in about 135 A.D.. Sinope is a city located on the southern shores the Black Sea. This information is available in Brown's, *Heresies,* and at www.didjesusexist.com/marcion.html.

All of these men were influenced by the Hellenistic thinking of their age, which was propagated and encouraged at Alexandria, Egypt. Alexandria was the home of the school of Philo, Ammonias Saccas, and Origen.[127] Philo, a Jew, is the progenitor of scholasticism, a mixture of Judaism and Greek philosophy.

10. The Gnostic Marcion

Marcion (70-150 AD), a rebellious son,[128] is one of the worst perverters of Scriptures. He is infamous for attempting to bribe the church at Rome. He concluded that the God of the OT was evil and the God of the NT was kind, benevolent, good, and "divine grace." Therefore, Marcion concluded there must be two Gods.

Marcion attacked the Canon of Scripture unmercifully.

> "Marcion dealt with the text of Paul's letters in the same way as with the text of Luke's gospel: anything which appeared inconsistent with what he believed to be authentic Pauline teaching was regarded as a corruption proceeding from an alien hand.'"[129]

Additionally, Marcion corrupted the Words of many verses in Luke and Paul's letters to weaken the connection with Judaism. For example,

> "In place of "Thy Kingdom Come" in the Lord's Prayer (Luke 11:2), Marcion's Gospel had the interesting variant:, 'Let thy Holy Spirit come on us and cleanse us.'"[130] "An example of a change reflecting Marcion's doctrine of God comes in Ephesians 3:9. The gospel there is described as 'the mystery hidden for ages *in* God who created all

---
[127] Brown, op. cit., pp. 17, 46 (*Heresies*).
[128] Ehrman; op. cit., p. 104 (*Lost Christianities*).
[129] Bruce, op. cit., p. 139 (*The Canon of Scripture*).
[130] Ibid. p. 138.

things'...to the mystery hidden for ages *from* the God who created all things.'"[131]

Marcion *constructed* two works. They are lost in antiquity, but a great deal is written about them, particularly in Irenaeus' *Against Heresies* and Tertullian's *Apology*. Marcion's works espoused *"another gospel"* [Gal. 1:6-9]. He is infamous to Bible-believers because he took a penknife to the Scriptures in the manner of King Jehoiakim [Jer. 36:23]. He mutilated the canonical gospels by removing entire chapters, changing or adding words as demonstrated above, and rejecting entire books. Similarly, Marcion discredited Paul's letters by accepting only ten (10) epistles and rejecting 1 and 2 Timothy and Titus. Allegedly, Marcion used only the gospel of Luke, whom he believed to be a Gentile, because he was bitterly anti-Semitic.[132] F. F. Bruce comments on this action by Marcion with the following remark, which contains the classic modernist's speculative terms, "possible" and "may have been." Dr. Bruce says:

> "It is **POSSIBLE** that the text of Luke which Marcion used as the basis for his *Gospel* was not identical with the text that has come down to us; it **MAY HAVE BEEN** an earlier edition, lacking the first two chapters—a sort of 'Proto-Luke'."[133]

It is comments like this from a known "great" and "wise" scholar [remember Job 32:8-9] that led others to "propose" a Q source document for the gospels as discussed below.

---

[131] Ibid. p. 141.
[132] Dr. Floyd Nolan Jones, *The Chronology of the Old Testament* (Master Books, Green Forrest, AR, 2005) 15, 18-19. Dr. Nolan presents compelling evidence that Luke was not a Gentile but a Jew.
[133] Bruce, op. cit. p. 137 (*The Canon of Scripture*).

There are presently many "Marcionites" in our schools, colleges, and universities around the world.

11. Other Gnostics

Valentinus (c. 105-165 A.D.), a Gnostic, was a contemporary of Marcion. He did not corrupt the Scriptures with a penknife, but rather he corrupted *individuals* by promoting his alleged "secret" insight into the gospels. He fashioned His *speculative* thoughts into a work called *The Gospel of Truth*. This is mentioned here because Tertullian (160-225 A.D.) reports that Valentinus used the "entire *instrumentum*."[134] In Tertullian's writings, *instrumentum* means the New Testament. This "flies in the face" of so many authors who claim there was no Canon because there was no "list" until very late.

12. Historical Information Thwarts Attempts to Undermine Scripture

Scholars claim the Muratorium Canon document (ca. 155-170), which gives a Canonical list, could not have listed a Canon of Scripture because, they insist, there was none. At this time, incredibly, to support their assertion, they have re-dated it from the 2nd century to the 4th century.[135] This is false. The overwhelming evidence from multiple sources concerning the recognized COS thwarts their attempt. There was a Canon of Scripture from the beginning. HEAR YE, HEAR YE, the Apostles and their companions or associates knew immediately that a book was canonical, which is defined as the inscripturated Words of

---

[134] Ibid. p. 145. (From Tertullian's, *Prescription*.).
[135] Ehrman, op. cit., p. 240-241 (*Lost Christianities*).

God. Do not be duped by *theorists* who suppress facts or by those who constantly redefine words, such as the Canon of Scripture. It is true that **some** churches considered **some** manuscripts "scripture" for a time. Nevertheless, the Holy Spirit influenced the Bible-believing churches to preserve the correct canonical Hebrew, Aramaic, and Greek books. The Scriptures indicate how their preservation would be accomplished. [Jn. 14:15, 23, 15:26, 16:13, Mat. 24:35, Rom. 3:1-2, 1 Tim. 3:15]

Ignatius (50-117 A.D.) quotes from numerous books of the COS. He does not cite which books, but how could he? Ignatius was on his way to be martyred in Rome without his parchments when he wrote his letters. He quotes from numerous books in the COS [see Appendix 2]. It is true that no early list of the books in the Canon has been found. Why? Because in a world with much fewer people, and certainly only a small remnant of poor, ragtag, often illiterate, believers, they knew which books were revered as the Words of God. Do you **list** the canonical books in your writings? It is not necessary because everyone knows. Well, early writers did not list them either.

In addition, Tertullian reports that the communication between churches and the travel between locations in the Roman Empire were much better than is usually believed.[136] They shared which books were accepted as canonical. Wilbur Pickering in his book, *The Identity of the New Testament Text,* reports that Gaius, the Apostle Paul's companion, had a collection of original canonical books called autographs [Acts 19:29, 20:4, 3 Jn. 1:1].[137]

If one does not ignore the early evidence, many authors present facts, references, and quotes, which affirm an early Canon of

---

[136] Williams, op. cit., p. *114* (*The Lie*).
[137] Pickering, op. cit., p. 116 (*The Identity of the New Testament Text*).

the Scriptures. They kept the list in their minds. It is sad that we need a written "list" in modern times because we do not have the list memorized. The gospels also were part of the early Canon.

Tatian's (110-180 A. D.) *Diatessaron* means "through the four." It is a borrowed musical *harmonic* term,[138] Tatian's work is a weaving of the four gospels. Although it is a corrupt work, it is another proof of books considered part of the early Canon.[139] Tatian was a student of Justin Martyr (c. 100-165 A.D.) at Rome.[140] Have you noted that all of these dates are RIGHT after the Revelator John wrote the last book of the Canon of Scripture in the early A.D. nineties of the first century?

Also, please note that there is no "conflict" between the gospels, but rather a harmony. Dr. Ehrman, who was trained at Princeton under the tutelage of the liberal scholar Bruce Metzger, views the Gospels as having multiple conflicts of facts in them.[141] This view has been repeatedly debunked through the centuries.

If someone desires to know the truth about the COS, the early date of the books, their preservation, and their recognitions, there is overwhelming evidence available today from multiple sources.

---

[138] Glen Davis, "The Development of the Canon of the New Testament, Peshitta," www.ntcanon.org/Peshitta.shtml. "The term diatesseron borrowed from musical terminology and designated a series of 4 harmonic tones."
[139] Metzger, op. cit., p. 313 (*The New Testament, Its Background, Growth, and Content*).
[140] Brown, op. cit., p. 77.
[141] Ehrman, op. cit., (*Lost Christianities*).

CHAPTER 7

A CANON WITHIN A CANON?

*"And as many as walk according to **this rule,** peace be on them, and mercy, and upon the Israel of God" Galatians 6:16.*

Along with the alleged late dating of the Canon,[142] scholars insist that church elders used apocryphal books as Scripture. They pound this fact to quell objections to reconsidering the recognized and accepted thirty-nine (39) canonical books of the Old Testament and twenty-seven (27) canonical books of the New Testament. In other words, they proclaim that there is really a **"canon within a canon"**[143] and that the present Canon should be extended to include many of the apocryphal books. They claim many other books should be included in a broader COS. Scholars are insisting that the Canon is still **open** and that some apocryphal books that are allegedly left out should be included in a broader COS.

As we saw earlier in this work, some scholars allege that "falsely" canonized books such as Revelation should be removed from the Canon of the New Testament.[144] Obviously, the book of Revelation is an embarrassment to the Roman Catholic Church, which can be easily identified in the Apocalypse. They also justify their claim to a **canon within a canon** by pointing to the Jewish canon as only a

---

[142] The only thing late about the canon is a "list" that "scholars" can hold in their hands.
[143] McDonald, op. cit., p. 3 (*The Canon Debate*).
[144] Ibid. p. 3.

part of the orthodox COS in the NT era.[145] In other words, they claim the Jews refuse to consider a broader canon, which would include the NT books, and similarly many Christians today are stubbornly refusing to consider a broader canon to include apocryphal books.

Be No More Children Tossed To and Fro

In their scenario, some of the apocryphal books would be admitted to the COS through their extension of the Canon to include the early works of competing *"Christianities."* In contrast, Jerome, (342-420 A.D.), who was much closer to the immediate post-Apostolic era, translated the apocryphal books for the *Latin Vulgate* as only of *historical* interest.

It was not until the Council of Trent (1545-1563 A.D.) that the apocryphal books were canonized for the Roman Catholics. Until recently, Baptists and Protestants were opposed to canonization of any other books. There is no reason for anyone but the scholars to believe pseudo-epigraphal Gnostic books recently uncovered at Nag Hammadi should be included in the COS. However, men like F. F. Bruce, Kurt Aland, Bruce Metzger, and dozens of other scholars, who deny the Canon is closed based on historical and Scriptural accounts (cf. 1 Cor. 13:9-12, Rev. 22:18-19), are having significant effects on the tide (or should I say the wind) of change.

Students of the ***received*** canonical Words proclaim:

> *That we henceforth be no more children, tossed to and fro, and carried about with every **wind** of doctrine, by the sleight of men, and cunning craftiness, whereby they lie in wait to deceive; [Ephes. 4:14] [my emphasis]*

---

[145] Ibid. pp. 15, 24-35. (*The Canon Debate*).

Chapter 7: A Canon Within a Canon?

In order to justify extending the COS, many authors report the apocryphal book, *Shepherd of Hermas,* was considered Scripture by Irenaeus and by Clement of Alexandria. Tertullian initially thought the book was canonical, but later rejected it.[146] However, the Muratorian Canon from the second century[147] does not list the *Shepherd of Hermas*. It does list the following: the four gospels, Acts, Paul's thirteen epistles, Jude, 1 and 2 John, and Revelation. It allegedly lists *The Wisdom of Solomon and The Apocalypse of Peter*, but decertifies *The Shepherd of Hermas*[148]. The history of the Muratorian Canon document certainly is intriguing and is suspect. Everyone must recognize that dealing with *pieces* of documents that are ancient is very difficult and fraught with danger. Too much can be read into them. Verifying their accuracy or the motivation of those who wrote them cannot be retroactively discovered or understood. Therefore, it is pure folly for scholars or for anyone to rely on them to develop scenarios, truths, stories, or recommendations. We must believe by faith in what God said He would do (Heb. 11:6); that is, preserve His truth [Psa 12:6-7, Mat. 24:35, 1 Pe. 1:23-25,] and guide believers into all Truth (Jn 16:13).

---

[146] Reference lost.
[147] "A reference to the episcopate of Pius at Rome ("nuperrime temporibus nostris") is usually taken to prove that the document cannot be later than *c.* 180, some 20 years after Pius's death (see *infra*)." www.earlychristianwritings.com/info/muratorian-wace.html.
[148] Ehrman, op. cit., p. 241 (*Lost Christianities*).

CHAPTER 8

THE GAME SCHOLARS PLAY

"Professing themselves to be wise, they became fools"
Romans 1:22.

At this point, a demonstration of the **_GAME_** played by modern Gnostics will be attempted. The following is a spoof to demonstrate how many Gnostic "scholars" write.

A Spoof

"**Could it be**" that Irenaeus' quote of the apocryphal book, *The Shepherd of Hermas*, is an "***insert***" into his writings in order to justify the elevation of that apocryphal book to Scripture? It is very **possible** that scholars from a certain denomination inserted the quote to justify other proposed recommended "adjustments" of the COS to remove the book of Revelation and insert *The Shepherd of Hermas*.

In the following quote attributed to Irenaeus, "**perhaps**" his sentences that quote *The Shepherd* are inserts. It would read better without it being present. An unknown editor, in order to justify the Shepherd of Hermas as Scripture by an *authoritative* synod or council, "**probably**" *inserted* it in Irenaeus' work, *Against Heresies*.

The following is the quote from Irenaeus' *Adversus Haereses*, chapter 20, Section 1-2:

> "For with Him were always present the Word and Wisdom, the son and the Spirit, by whom and in whom, freely and spontaneously, He made all things, to whom also He speaks, saying, "Let Us make man after Our

image and likeness," (1) He taking from Himself the substance of the creatures [formed], and the pattern of things made, and the type of all the adornments in the world.

The next italicized, bolded sentences in Irenaeus' work following the quote above are the alleged quote of *The Shepherd of Hermas* by Irenaeus:

> ***Truly, then, the Scripture declared, which says,***
> ***"First (2) of all believe that there is one God, who has established all things, and completed them, and having caused that from what had no being, all things should come into existence: He who contains all things and is Himself contained by no one."***
> Rightly also has Malachi said among the prophets: "Is it not one God who hath established us? Have we not all one Father? (3)..."[149]

What is "*obvious*" pertains to the bolded, indented quote, which is an insert. Take it out and the passage reads better. THE END OF THIS SPOOF.

Redefining Words

The modern "scholar" would subsequently conclude that Irenaeus' quote is truly an obvious insert into the text. The preceding is the way 'scholars' frequently reason. The truth is nobody knows. You cannot base prima facie evidence on speculation, possibilities, probabilities, perhaps, maybe, etc.

---

[149] Irenaeus, *Against Heresies (Adversus Haereses);* from an online translation at www.ccel.org/fathers/ANF-01/iren/iren4.html#Section20. Accessed March, 2004.

F. F. Bruce attempts to explain away the *Shepherd of Hermas* quote by Irenaeus by suggesting the definition of "scripture" used by early writers was very broad.[150] It is difficult for this writer to accept that early writers had a casual approach to calling many writings Scripture. A review of the Greek word, γραθη, graphe translated Scripture in the COS reveals a very specific use of the term.

Inserts?

We see repeated attempts in the works of modernists to degrade the preserved verbal and plenary Scriptures by innuendos and false assertions, or probabilities and speculation. A few facts are turned into a textbook of concocted stories. A classic example will be offered from *Lost Christianities*. Note the allusion to "inserts."

Dr Ehrman says:

> "...most critical SCHOLARS THINK THAT 1 Timothy is pseudonymous...but what about the passage in 1 Corinthians? No one doubts that Paul wrote that letter. Even so, there are good reasons for thinking Paul did **NOT** write the passage about women being silent in chapter 14. For one thing, just three chapters earlier Paul condoned the practice of women speaking in church. They are to have their heads covered, he insists, when they pray and

---

[150] Bruce, op. cit., p. 29 (*The Canon of Scripture*). The correct approach to Irenaeus' use of *The Shepherd of Hermas* as Scripture is this: "when we speak of 'the scriptures' we mean 'the sacred writings' as distinct from other writings: to us 'scripture' and 'writing' are separated words with distinct meanings. But in Hebrew and Greek one and the same word does duty for both 'writing' and scripture': in these languages 'the scriptures' are simply 'the writings'—that is today, 'the writings' *par excellence*." The conclusion is that if Irenaeus used the word Scripture, he may or may not have meant that the writing was sacred. In other words, Irenaeus used the word scripture to refer to canonical as well as other respected writings. So, in Irenaeus' quote above, substitute "writing" for Scripture.

> prophecy—activities done out loud in antiquity. How could Paul condone a practice (women speaking in church) in chapter 11 that he condemns in chapter 14?
>
> "It has often been noted that the passage in chapter 14 also APPEARS intrusive in its own literary context: Both before and after his instructions for women to keep silent, Paul is speaking not about women in church but about prophets in church. When the verses on women **ARE REMOVED,** the passage flows neatly without a break. This too **SUGGESTS** that these verses were **INSERTED** into the passage later. Moreover, it is striking that the verses in question appear in different locations in some of our surviving manuscripts of Paul's letter as if they had originally appeared as a marginal note (drawn from the teaching of the forged letter of 1 Timothy?) and **INSERTED** as judged appropriate in different parts of the chapter. **ON THESE GROUNDS**, a number of scholars have concluded that Paul's instructions for women to be silent in 1 Corinthians **MAY NOT BE** from Paul, just as the letter to Timothy is not from Paul.[151] [my emphasis, HDW]

Is the passage an insert or not an insert? God knows and that is why we must trust Him. His words command our trust and faith [Rom. 14:23, Heb. 11:6]. Their application to life demands our recognition of their truthfulness. He said, *"Heaven and earth shall pass away: but my words shall not pass away"* [Lk. 21:33]. From this verse alone it is clear that His Words would be preserved [cf. Psa. 12:6-7; Mat. 5:17-18, 24:35] and they would be pure [Psa. 12:6-7, Pro. 30:5].

Q Document?

Another example of speculation by modernistic Gnostic scholars will be offered before presenting the effects of all this ballyhoo and ilk. In Dr. Ehrman's book, he relates the well-known ***theory*** about

---

[151] Ehrman, op. cit., p. 138 (*Lost Christianities*).

Chapter 8: The Games Scholars Play

the Q document.[152] Q comes from the German word, Quelle, meaning source. The Germans **proposed** a common source for the synoptic gospels, "a solution that is still held by the majority of researchers today."[153] A few paragraphs later on the next page, Dr. Ehrman speaks of the Q document as if it existed, as if it had been found and could be read. He says:

> "A large number of the sayings in Q are not in Thomas [He is referring to the non-canonical Gospel of Thomas], and a number of the sayings in Thomas are not in Q. but they may have been similar documents with comparable theological views."[154] [my addition, HDW]

How can he be so dogmatic in this quote, which flatly indicates the Q document is a real entity rather than a theory?[155] He is working with circumstantial evidence that can be interpreted in many ways. The correct view is that Thomas copied from the Scripture. There is no document or manuscript that has been found which can be called "Q." There is only speculation.

---

[152] Cloud, op. cit. p. 303 (Way of Life Encyclopedia). The modernistic theory of a Q document is one aspect of *form* or *redaction* criticism.
[153] Ibid. p. 57.
[154] Ibid. p. 58.
[155] Another example of modernistic textual critics turning a **theory** into a dogmatic fact can be found referenced in Wilbur Pickering's *The Identity of the New Testament Text*, pp. 37-38. Pickering reports Hort's Lucian recension **theory** has been picked up as **"dogmatic"** truth by some **"scholars."** They also claim a recension for the Peshitta Syrian text since it attests to the Traditional Text. p. 38.

CHAPTER 9

SCHOLARS WANT TO CHANGE THE BIBLE

"For I testify unto every man that heareth the words of the prophecy of this book, If any man shall add unto these things, God shall add unto him the plagues that are written in this book: And if any man shall take away from the words of the book of this prophecy, God shall take away his part out of the book of life, and out of the holy city, and from the things which are written in this book" Revelation 22:18-19.

Add to or Reduce the Canon?

What is the attack on the Canon of Scripture all about? There are many reasons for the attack from authority to pedantic scholarship, to hate, to greed, to pride, etc. However, the clearest reason is revealed in a recent book, *The Canon Debate*. The editors state:

> More than a generation ago, Kurt Aland raised the question of reducing the biblical canon by omitting works that some scholars consider to be an embarrassment to the majority of the church, for example, the apocalyptic literature of the New Testament (2 Peter, Revelation, etc.) in order TO PROMOTE CHRISTIAN UNITY. [Kurt Aland, *The Problem of the New Testament Canon*(London: Mowbray, 1962). 28-33] Not long after that Ernst Käsemann also asked whether there should be a "CANON WITHIN THE CANON"—in essence, a reduction of the biblical text—in order to alleviate concerns over the diversity within the Bible. [Ernst Käsemann, *The Canon of the New Testament Church and the Unity of the Church*, (London: SCM, 1968), 95-107]...Metzger contends that

> although in principle the Bible canon MAY BE CHANGED, in all practicality any changes in the present Christian Bible would undoubtedly cause more, not less division in the church. [B. M. Metzger, *The Canon of the New Testament: Its Origin, Development, and Significance* (Oxford: Clarendon, 1987), 275][156]

Will This Achieve Unity?

The bottom line is that many scholars are trying to achieve *unity* and *tolerance,* a noble cause, by just the opposite of what would be achieved by these *idealist* goals. Unity is achieved by belief in every Word of the Scriptures and not by removing Words, passages, books of the COS or by casting doubt on them. Certainly, casting doubt on the foundational document of the world by speculative philosophy and reasoning will unsettle the very fabric of civilization. World and national stats reveal that this is beginning to happen [See the graphs in the appendices]. At the end of his book, *Lost Christianities,* Bart Ehrman reflects on the "Christian tradition" and other "views" that are "truths." He proposes his thoughts on religion, which reflect his idealistic and humanistic approach. The statement that stands out most, however, is:

Tolerance?

> "For good or ill, there is a greater sense—though obviously not a universal sense—of the need for tolerance."[157]

His idea of "tolerance" is acceptance of his ideas or "anything" other than the acceptance of the canonical books of the Bible. Dr.

---

[156] McDonald, op. cit., pp. 3-4 (*The Canon Debate*).
[157] Ehrman, op. cit., p. 256 (*Lost Christianities*).

Ehrman knows that he would have to come under the authority of an Almighty God if he accepts the preserved canonical Words. What about accepting God's ideas as found in His preserved Words and not in mine, not in scholars, and certainly not in his writings? [Mat. 4:4, 24:35, Lk. 4:4, 1 Pe. 1:23-25, Psa 12:6-7]

In contradistinction to most modern scholars, Bible-believing Christians believe that all truth was given by God in a book:

1. that has been providentially preserved and protected from attacks,
2. that reflects a miraculous unity in sixty-six books written by forty plus authors guided by the Holy Spirit, and
3. that has astounded many very brilliant men throughout the centuries [Job 32:8-9].

Instead of attacking the Bible, they should be enjoined by it and come under its authority. There is no way for *"desperately wicked"* and philosophical men to declare what is foundational for teaching, preaching, and the way of life [Jer. 17:9]. This theme, this truth, permeates the Scripture. It is confirmed by an honest and forthright look back at history. We will return to this in a moment. First, let us examine a scenario that portends just good ol' common sense.

CHAPTER 10

An Allegory

Let us propose that the scholars at a major university[158] decided to contend with a set of documents establishing the rules or canon for management of the institution. The administration had published its conditions for employment and administration of the faculty, of the students, and of the campus many years ago. However, the "scholars" on campus had examined the document and decided that much of it was probably fraudulent. At the very least, it had "inserts" that confused some employees and embarrassed others. There were many rules in the document, such as dress codes for women, doctrines of separation, and warnings not to change the document. The canons (rules) for administration were significantly different from what was desired by the teachers and students in modern times.

The "staff" in a previous or earlier administration warned that any changes to the wording of the document would bring disasters. No one is quite sure who wrote the document. A scholarly search for old "proto-documents" was made. Some were found in garbage dumps, some were found on dusty shelves, some were found in former rebellious professor's files, and some were presented to the scholars as "the oldest and best," but they were obviously corrupted. The scholars suggested reconstructing a document based upon genealogical comparisons and their choices for the most likely wording of the

---

[158] Fenton John Anthony Hort (April 23, 1828 - November 30, 1892). "During his time there he took part in discussions on university reform" Hort is another who is never satisfied with "authority." Quote from www.fact-index.com/f/fe/fenton_john_anthony_hort.html.

original documents. An evaluation of all the sources showed that PERHAPS there had been many changes in the original documents. Previous scholars, who were not satisfied with the administration's rules or canon, PROBABLY made the alterations. Furthermore, scholars and archaeologists found documents of "proto-groups," who had lost previous battles for control and authority.

Nevertheless, one small group of professors on campus, called the DBS, maintained the document was correct as written based upon the fact that the vast majority of supporting documents were virtually identical. But all the other groups of scholars scoffed at them

The "scholars" recommended removing some parts of the canon on the basis that those parts were most likely corrupted by previous administrations to maintain control. No one was completely convinced that this should be done, but they reasoned that it would demonstrate tolerance of other groups.

Some "scholars" alleged that previous malcontents bent on achieving power most likely inserted various parts of the ancient document. Great controversies arose. Factions became angry over differing proposals and recommendations. The most disconcerting observation, however, was that no one had noticed the significant change in the children attending the university. The students on campus decided that there were **PROBABLY** no absolute standards, canon, or rules ever made because of all the confusion generated by the warring scholars.

Slowly, but surely, the students became rebellious. Riots broke out on the streets. The students decided there was no real foundational document and that, if there ever was one, no one knew what it really said. Sexual misconduct and exposed body parts became the norm on campus. The current administration acquiesced to the request for coed dorms. The incidences of venereal disease soared. Unwanted pregnancies occurred. The number of abortions soared. Cheating and prevarication became acceptable. Suicides rates and crime stats steadily climbed. Graduates of the university obtained jobs in foundational industries of the nation. Their rejection of authority, morality, and truthfulness caused business failures. Some of the university graduates went to jail. Their marriages crumbled. Divorce rates soared. Some of their children became school shooters. Church attendance plummeted.[159]

Yet, the "scholars" continued to argue and debate the foundational document for the university. They quibbled over "jots and tittles," sections, and chapters; all the while oblivious to the deterioration around them, or blaming it on "families," or the lack of national laws and security, or too many laws, or technology, or the courts, or always on someone or something else, but never on themselves. Eventually, the foundations of the nation were destroyed and the nation crumbled from within.

Finally, an *"Ancient of Days"* returned and affirmed the document was right all along. The "scholars" had simply woven a tale from a few facts into an imaginary scenario. However, it was too late. The end had come. The "Ancient of Days" said, **"Have ye not read?"** [Mat. 22:31] **"It is written,"** [Mat 4:4, and 93 other places]

> *The eyes of the Lord **preserve knowledge**, and he overthroweth the words of the transgressor. [Proverbs 22:12]*

> **Have not I written** *to thee excellent things in counsels and knowledge, [21] That I might make thee know the certainty of **the words of truth**; that thou mightest*

---

[159] See Appendix 4.

*answer **the words of truth** to them that send unto thee? [Proverbs 22:20-21]*

All scripture is given by inspiration of God, and is profitable for doctrine, for reproof, for correction, for instruction in righteousness: That the man of God may be perfect, throughly furnished unto all good works. [2 Tim. 3:16-17]

Now I beseech you, brethren, mark them which cause divisions and offences contrary to the doctrine which ye have learned; and avoid them. 18For they that are such serve not our Lord Jesus Christ, but their own belly; and by good words and fair speeches deceive the hearts of the simple. [Romans 16:17-18]

For such are false apostles, deceitful workers, transforming themselves into the apostles of Christ. 14And no marvel; for Satan himself is transformed into an angel of light. 15Therefore it is no great thing if his ministers also be transformed as the ministers of righteousness; whose end shall be according to their works. [2 Cor. 11:13-15]

The heart is deceitful above all things, and desperately wicked: who can know it? [Jeremiah 17:9]

The words of the LORD are pure words: as silver tried in a furnace of earth, purified seven times. 7Thou shalt keep them, O LORD, thou shalt preserve them from this generation for ever. [Psalm 12:6-7]

Heaven and earth shall pass away, but my words shall not pass away. [Matthew 24:35]

For verily I say unto you, Till heaven and earth pass, one jot or one tittle shall in no wise pass from the law, till all be fulfilled. [Mat. 5:18]

Chapter 10: An Allegory

For all flesh is as grass, and all the glory of man as the flower of grass. The grass withereth, and the flower thereof falleth away: 25But the word of the Lord endureth for ever. And this is the word which by the gospel is preached unto you. [1 Peter 1:24-25]

My covenant will I not break, nor alter the thing that is gone out of my lips. [Psalm 89:34]

Know therefore that the LORD thy God, he is God, the faithful God, which keepeth covenant and mercy with them that love him and keep his commandments to a thousand generations; [Deut. 7:9]

The counsel of the LORD standeth for ever, the thoughts of his heart to all generations. [Psalm 33:11]

For ever, O LORD, thy word is settled in heaven. [Psalm 119:89]

The earth also is defiled under the inhabitants thereof; because they have transgressed the laws, changed the ordinance, broken the everlasting covenant. [Isaiah 24:5]

I will worship toward thy holy temple, and praise thy name for thy lovingkindness and for thy truth: for thou hast magnified thy word above all thy name. [Psalm 138:2]

For whatsoever things were written aforetime were written for our learning, that we through patience and comfort of the scriptures might have hope. [Romans 15:4]

For I testify unto every man that heareth the words of the prophecy of this book, If any man shall add unto these things, God shall add unto him the plagues that are written in this book: 19And if any man shall take away from the words of the book of this prophecy, God shall take away his part out of the book of life, and out of the holy city, and from the things which are written in this book. [Rev. 22:18-19]

And if any man hear my words, and believe not, I judge him not: for I came not to judge the world, but to save the world. 48He that rejecteth me, and receiveth not my words, hath one that judgeth him: the word that I have spoken, the same shall judge him in the last day. [John 12:47-48]

Because sentence against an evil work is not executed speedily, therefore the heart of the sons of men is fully set in them to do evil. [Eccles. 8:11]

God forbid: yea, let God be true, but every man a liar; as it is written, That thou mightest be justified in thy sayings, and mightest overcome when thou art judged. [Romans 3:4]

CHAPTER 11

CONCLUSION

*"And he shall turn the heart of the fathers to the children, and the heart of the children to their fathers, lest I come and SMITE the earth with **A** curse [cherem]" Malachi 4:6. [my emphasis and additions, HDW]*

The Curse

This author has often wondered what THE curse in Malachi could be. The verse plainly says **A** curse, not curses. God uses the Hebrew word cherem for curse in Malachi 4:6:

WHAT IS **THE** CURSE? An attempt shall be made to answer the question. This author believes the answer has great significance because it relates to the modernist textual critic destroying the very foundations of society and leading our children astray, particularly in America, but yet, around the world.

It is fascinating in this verse in Malachi that God chose to use the Hebrew word cherem. It is used elsewhere as a "devoted thing." For example in Lev. 27:28:

> *Notwithstanding no devoted thing [cherem], that a man shall devote unto the LORD of all that he hath, both of man and beast, and of the field of his possession, shall be sold or redeemed: every devoted thing [cherem] is most holy unto the LORD.*

And in Num. 18:14:

Every thing devoted [cherem] in Israel shall be thine.

God seems to be saying in Mal. 4:6 that He will **smite** the earth [meaning nations] with *a devoted thing*. What could *the devoted thing* be in Malachi or the thing that should be devoted but is not, and is the reason for smiting the nations? God mentions the relationship between fathers and children in the first part of the verse. Does the curse have something to do with our children? Could this "curse" that God warned He would send upon the earth be related to a devoted thing, "our children?" Recent social stats confirm that we are suffering from or being smitten by what should be *a devoted thing, OUR CHILDREN*.

The stats in Africa, concerning the parentless children running amuck because of the death of their parents secondary to AIDS, are frightening. A missionary in Africa for over forty years recently stayed at our home. Shortly before coming to the U.S. on furlough, he reports that his wife was attacked and severely beaten. He said that they had to be in their home, fortified with iron bars, before 4 PM every day or risk being beaten or murdered by children. One day his wife was late getting home...

The stats in America, and for that matter around the world, reflect this same curse, the *"cherem,"* the "devoted" thing, running amuck. The evidence is non-controvertible. Just go to the Josephson Institute reports, or to the Barna website, or look at the Department of Justice graphs in *The Lie That Changed The Modern World* published by Bible For Today [some of the graphs are reproduced in the appendices].

Warnings

Are there other passages of Scripture that suggest the curse in Malachi 4:6 refers to our children, "no longer devoted things," which have become a curse? Hosea sounded the alarm. But, before proceeding, remember what Paul said in Romans 15:4a:

"For whatsoever things were written aforetime were written for our learning,"

In the following presentation from Scripture, my comments are in the brackets and are not italicized. Hosea 4:1-12 says:

*Hear **the word of the Lord** [the inscripturated words], ye children of Israel: for the Lord hath a controversy with the inhabitants of the land, because **there is no truth**, nor mercy, **nor knowledge of God in the land*** [because the canon and textual critics have destroyed confidence in the foundation, and the apostates have infiltrated our schools.]

[2] By swearing, and lying, and killing, and stealing, and committing adultery, they break out, and blood toucheth blood. [Crime stats are increasing, which includes murder, rape, theft, divorce often due to adultery, and violence in schools] *[3] Therefore shall the land mourn, and every one that dwelleth therein shall languish, with the beasts of the field, and with the fowls of heaven; yea, the fishes of the sea also shall be taken away.* [Environmental research reports a marked decrease in schools of fish.]

*[4] Yet let no man strive, nor reprove another: for thy people are as they that strive with **the priest**.* [An intermediary between God and man] *[5] Therefore shalt thou fall in the day, and **the prophet*** [the preacher who brings Gods words to the people] *also shall fall with thee in the night, and **I will destroy thy mother**.* [Divorce and abortions wreak havoc on mothers]

[6] My people are destroyed for lack of knowledge [the Scriptures]: *because thou hast rejected knowledge* [Many have rejected God's preserved Words which we are to receive], *I will also reject thee, that thou shalt be no priest to me* [that the priesthood of believers, the royal priesthood, is being diminished, is uncontestable.]: *seeing* **thou hast forgotten** *the law of thy God* [Not only have we forgotten, but our educators blaspheme the preserved, pure, eternal words of God.], ***I WILL ALSO FORGET THY CHILDREN***

[7] As they [the children, (see JFB in the footnote)[160]] *were increased, so they sinned against me: therefore will I change their glory* [Proverbs 17:6 Children's children are the crown of old men; and THE GLORY OF CHILDREN ARE THEIR FATHERS] *into shame.* [Father's are being shamed all over the world. Which father could watch someone's nude daughter prancing around on stage or view pornographic pictures of daughters in cyberspace, displayed for millions to see?] *[8] They* [thy children] *eat up the sin of my people* [the children relish sin such as pornography, adultery, murder, stealing, and prevarication] *and they* [the children] *set their heart on their iniquity* [self-will].

[9] And there shall be, like people, like priest: and I will punish them for their ways, and reward them their doings. [The people and priest shall be like the children] *[10] For they shall eat, and not have enough: they shall commit whoredom, and shall not increase: because they have left off to take heed to the Lord.* [to hearken unto His preserved Words, which are precepts, commands, judgments, statutes, laws, etc. to protect us]

[11] Whoredom and wine and new wine take away the heart. [Alcoholism, and drug abuse (pharmacopoeia) is

---

[160] Jameson, Fausett, Brown, Ho 4:7. As they were increased--in numbers and power. Compare Ho 4:6, **"thy children," to which their "increase" in numbers refers**. so they sinned--(Compare Ho 10:1; 13:6). will I change their glory into shame--that is, I will strip them of all they now glory in (their numbers and power), and give them shame instead. A just retribution: as they changed their glory into shame, by idolatry (Ps 106:20; Jer 2:11; Ro 1:23; Php 3:19).

rampant.] *[12] My people ask counsel at their stocks* [their idols, which may include the stock market rather than the words of God], *and their staff declareth unto them* [Their idols, their channelers, their horoscopes]: *for the spirit of whoredoms hath caused them to err, and they have gone a whoring from* **under their God** [which is **the authority** of the preserved, inerrant, plenary Words of God]. [my additions in brackets, HDW]

The Answer

Jeremiah has the answer to all these problems, and this most serious curse that has come upon the earth.

Jer 3:19 says:

*But I said, How shall I put thee AMONG THE CHILDREN, and give thee a pleasant land, a goodly heritage of the hosts of nations? and I said, Thou shalt call me, My father; and shalt **not** turn away from me.* [shalt not turn away from His words, HDW]

But the hydra continues to grow new heads. How can doom and destruction be avoided? Surely, the storm clouds are on the horizon. This author personally believes that the "earth" (THE NATIONS) will not turn back to a sure foundation, the living Words of a loving, living God full of mercy and grace. The evidence is all too clear as to which path the nations are taking.

Remember His Words

What happens when God "forgets" a nation? When God forgets our children? [Hosea 6:4]. The enemy comes in like a flood [Psa 90:3-8; Isa 59:19]. Without a doubt the enemy now influences our children.

When God hides His face from our children, the blessings of a nation are withdrawn [Psa 104:29].

When the bread from heaven, the manna, by which man shall **not** live without is not RECEIVED daily [Mat. 4:4, Lk. 4:4], when man does not trust that he will be provided bread daily [Mat. 6:8], when man collects corrupted manna from far and wide, from monasteries, from caves, and from Vatican shelves, **then man's supply of bread becomes corrupted, spoiled, or infected and:**

A little leaven leaveneth the whole lump. Galatians 5:9

God has provided America with water, manna, and land: *"That they might observe his statutes, and keep his laws."* [Psalm 105:45] Rather, *"Yea, they despised the pleasant land, THEY BELIEVED NOT HIS WORD:"* [Psalm 106:24] They have *"murmured in their tents, and hearkened not unto the voice of the Lord."* [Psalm 106:25] They have murmured with excitement about manuscripts found in graves, garbage dumps, and on the shelves of the enemy, and when a nation acts so unrighteous, the Palmist says, *"Therefore he [God] lifted up his hand against them, to overthrow them in the wilderness:"* [Psalm 106:26]. But what is IGNORED by so many of us is the next verse,

> *To overthrow THEIR SEED [THEIR CHILDREN] also among the nations, and to scatter them in the lands. [Psalm 106:27] [My addition, HDW]*

God goes on to say:

> *They joined themselves also unto Baal-peor, and ate the sacrifices of the dead. [29] Thus they provoked him to anger with THEIR INVENTIONS: and the plague brake in upon them. [30] Then stood up Phinehas, and executed judgment: and so the plague was stayed. [31] And that*

> *was counted unto him for righteousness unto all generations for evermore. [Psalm 106:28-31] [my emphasis, HDW]*

Let us pray that more of us will be a Phinehas and stay the plague, the curse, *"the devoted thing,"* that is upon us. We are sacrificing our sons and daughters unto devils. [Psa 106:37] Devils are influencing our educational system and here is the proof.

In a recent book, *Lost Christianities*, written by Bart Ehrman, Chair of the Department of Religious Studies at the University of North Carolina in Chapel Hill, Dr Ehrman wrote the following words,

> As we will see, these confrontations were waged largely on literary grounds, as members of the proto-orthodox group produced polemical tractates in opposition to other Christian perspectives, FORGED SACRED TEXTS to provide authorization for their own perspectives (FORGERIES, THAT IS, CLAIMING TO BE WRITTEN BY JESUS OWN APOSTLES), AND COLLECTED OTHER EARLY WRITINGS INTO A SACRED CANON OF SCRIPTURE TO ADVANCE <u>THEIR VIEWS</u> and counteract the views of others. It is out of these conflicts that the New Testament came into being, a collection of twenty-seven books <u>TAKEN TO BE SACRED, INSPIRED, and AUTHORITATIVE.</u>[161] [My emphasis, but **not** my addition in parentheses, which is Dr. Ehrman's statement.]

In other words, Dr. Ehrman, a teacher of college students, our children, has belittled the verbal, plenary, inspired, preserved Canon of Scripture and the priesthood of believers, who have guarded, protected, and preserved God's words by their very lives.[162] It bears

---

[161] Ehrman, op. cit. p. 7 (*Lost Christianities*). Dr. Ehrman continues by supplying his readers with a list of forged canonical books in the remainder of his book that can only be characterized by Paul's statement in Gal. 2:8.
[162] Braght, op. cit. pp. 5-60 (*Martyrs Mirror*).

repeating that the registrar at the University of North Carolina reports the average number of students that graduate per year from UNC at Chapel Hill is 6,579. Each student is required to take a philosophy or religion course. Dr. Ehrman's writings are chipping away at the very foundations, and influencing our children, claiming to establish truth by "perhaps," "maybe," "could be," etc.[163]

God continued His discussion about the rejection of His words in Psalm 106 with these words:

> *Yea, **they sacrificed their sons and their daughters** unto devils, [38] And shed innocent blood, even the blood of their sons and of their daughters, whom they sacrificed unto the idols of Canaan: and the land was polluted with blood. [39] Thus were they defiled with their own works, and went a whoring WITH THEIR OWN INVENTIONS. [40] Therefore was the wrath of the Lord kindled against his people, insomuch that he abhorred his own inheritance. [41] And he gave them into the hand of the heathen; and they that hated them ruled over them. [42] Their enemies also oppressed them, and they were brought into subjection under their hand. [Psalm 106:37-42]*

Brothers and Sisters, WE MUST CRY OUT IN PRAYER TO SAVE OUR CHILDREN. Our God is merciful and full of grace. The Psalmist said:

---

[163] God hates "Humanism." In Isaiah 2:22 He says, "Cease ye from man," and in 3:4 says if you do not, ..."I will give *children to be their princes and babes shall rule over them....the child shall behave himself proudly against the ancient, and the base against the honorable."* Has anyone else noted the attitude of many of the young in America?

Chapter 11: Conclusion

"Nevertheless he regarded their affliction, when he heard their cry"

[Psalm 106:44].

H. D. Williams, M. D., Ph.D.

APPENDICES

APPENDIX 1

Robert Dick Wilson

Robert Dick Wilson was truly a remarkable gentleman. Bible students are indebted to him for the masterful work he did in helping to confirm the credibility of the Old Testament. Robert Wilson was born in 1856; he graduated from Princeton University at the age of twenty. He went on to earn both a Masters degree and a Ph.D. He then did further post-graduate work in Germany for two years. He was a brilliant language student - when he was still in college, he could read his New Testament in nine languages. Wilson was but twenty-five years of age when he determined that he would invest years of careful study in the text of the Old Testament, so that he could speak with authority as to whether or not it has been preserved in an accurate format. The body of Old Testament literature was completed by 400 B.C., and yet, prior to 1946 (when the Dead Sea scrolls were discovered), the oldest copies of the Old Testament Scriptures we possessed dated to about the 10th century A.D. There was, therefore, a gap of some 1,200 years between the last of the Old Testament books, and the extant manuscripts. Could we be sure that the writings at our disposal had been faithfully preserved? After all, even if one is confident that the original Scriptures were inspired of God, that would amount to little if they have been grossly corrupted across the centuries. This was the task, therefore, to which young Wilson dedicated himself. And he was a wonderfully disciplined person. Based upon the longevity of his immediate ancestors, Robert Wilson estimated that he might live to about seventy years of age. Since he was twenty-five at the time, that would give him about forty-five years remaining to accomplish his goal. Accordingly, he divided his projected remaining years into three periods of fifteen years each. Here is how he would pursue his plan. For the first fifteen years, he would study every language that had a bearing on the text of the Old Testament. He set himself to the task. During that time he mastered *forty-five languages!* He not only became an expert in Hebrew, and its kindred tongues, but he learned all the languages into which the Scriptures had been translated down to the year A.D. 600. During the next fifteen years Wilson dedicated himself to studying the text of the Old Testament itself. He looked at every consonant in the Old Testament text (the Hebrew Old Testament has no vowels) - about *one and a quarter million* of them. He made a thorough scientific investigation of the Old Testament text, as compared to other writings of antiquity. Wilson noted that there are twenty-nine ancient, pagan kings of various nations which are mentioned in the Bible. Their names are also found in the writings of their own lands. The names of these kings consist of 195 consonants. He discovered that in the Old Testament, there are only two or three of the letters - of the entire 195 - that are in question as to spelling. By way of contrast, in the secular literature of the same period, the names of those rulers frequently are so garbled that one can scarcely identify the person. For example, Ptolemy, an ancient writer, drew up a list of eighteen Babylonian kings, and not a one of them is spelled correctly. The text of the Bible was amazingly precise. Wilson then spent his remaining years writing down the results of his long research. He authored a marvelous book titled, *A Scientific Investigation of the Old Testament,* in which he confidently affirmed "we are scientifically certain that we have substantially the same [Old Testament] text that was in the possession of Christ and the apostles and, so far as anybody knows, the same as that written by the original composers of the Old Testament documents." We ought to be grateful for those who have gone before us, and who have provided us with evidence for the integrity of the biblical text. By the way, Wilson died at the age of seventy-four.[164]

---

[164] Jackson, Wayne; "The Remarkable Robert Dick Wilson," *Christian Courier*, Penpoints, Monday, April 24, 2000. (www.christiancourier.com/penpoints/rdWilson.htm).

APPENDIX 2

Cross Reference Table: Early Writings That Confirm the COS [165]

Each symbol in the large table below corresponds to a specific authority and a specific writing. The symbols summarize the opinion of the authority about the writing. The symbols have this meaning:

Symbol	Opinion of Authority
√	accepted; true; scriptural; or quoted from very approvingly
◊	possible approving quotation or allusion
±	acceptable, but only with changes
?	dubious; disputed; or useful for inspiration
¿	spurious (in the classification of Eusebius)
x	false; heretical; heterodox; quoted from very disapprovingly
·	not mentioned or quoted from; opinion unknown

<u>Early</u> Writings of Christian Authorities, Referenced in the Next Chart, Confirm the COS as Opposed to the Apocrypha

Ignatius of Antioch (35-107 A.D.)
Polycarp of Smyrna (69-155 A.D.
Marcion (70-150 A.D.)
Valentinus (105-165 A.D.)
Justin Martyr (100-165 A.D.)
Irenaeus of Lyons (120-192 A.D.)
Clement of Alexandria (150-217 A.D.)
Tertullian of Carthage (150-220 A.D.)

---

[165] Glen Davis. These excellent tables are used with permission from Brother Davis. The html links were removed to reduce the size of the document, but a visit to the site and links is very worthwhile. http://www.ntcanon.org/table.shtml

Muratorian Canon (c. 200 A.D.)
Origen (184-254 A.D.)
Eusebius of Caesarea (260-340 A.D.)
codex Sinaiticus (c. 4th century)
Athanasius of Alexandria (296-373 A.D.)
Didymus the Blind (313-398 A.D.)
Peshitta (c. 442 A.D.)
Vulgate (405 A.D.)

	Ig	Po	M	Va	JM	Ir	C	T	MC	O	E	CS	A	D	P	V
Gospel according to Matthew	√	√	¿	√	√	√	√	√	√	√	√	√	√	√	√	√
Gospel according to Mark	.	√	.	√	√	√	√	√	√	√	√	√	√	√	√	√
Gospel according to Luke	√	√	±	√	√	√	√	√	√	√	√	√	√	√	√	√
Gospel according to John	.	.	x	√	√	√	√	√	√	√	√	√	√	√	√	√
Acts	√	√	x	.	.	√	√	√	√	√	√	√	√	√	√	√
Romans	√	√	±	√	.	√	√	√	√	√	√	√	√	√	√	√
I Corinthians	√	√	±	√	.	√	√	√	√	√	√	√	√	√	√	√
II Corinthians	.	√	±	√	.	√	√	√	√	√	√	√	√	√	√	√
Galatians	.	√	±	√	.	√	√	√	√	√	√	√	√	√	√	√
Ephesians	√	√	±	√	.	√	√	√	√	√	√	√	√	√	√	√
Philippians	.	√	±	√	.	√	√	√	√	√	√	√	√	√	√	√
Colossians	√	.	±	√	.	√	√	√	√	√	√	√	√	√	√	√
I Thessalonians	√	√	±	.	.	√	√	√	√	√	√	√	√	√	√	√
II Thessalonians	.	√	±	.	.	√	√	√	√	√	√	√	√	√	√	√
I Timothy	.	√	x	.	.	√	√	√	√	√	√	√	√	√	√	√
II Timothy	.	√	x	.	.	√	√	√	√	√	√	√	√	√	√	√

The Attack on the Canon of Scripture

Book																
Titus	.	.	x	.	.	√	√	√	√	√	√	√	√	√	√	√
Philemon	.	.	±	.	.	.	.	√	√	√	√	√	√	.	√	√
Hebrews	.	.	.	.	.	◊	√	√	.	√	√	√	√	√	√	√
James	.	.	.	.	.	◊	.	.	.	?	?	√	√	√	√	√
I Peter	.	√	.	√	.	√	√	√	.	√	√	√	√	√	√	√
II Peter	.	.	.	.	.	.	.	.	.	?	?	√	√	√	.	√
I John	.	√	.	√	.	√	√	√	√	√	√	√	√	√	√	√
II John	.	.	.	.	.	√	.	.	√	?	?	√	√	x	.	√
III John	.	√	.	.	.	.	.	.	.	?	?	√	√	x	.	√
Jude	.	.	.	.	.	.	√	√	√	√	?	√	√	√	.	√
Revelation of John	.	.	.	√	√	√	√	√	√	√	√	√	√	√	.	√
Gospel of Thomas	.	.	.	.	.	.	.	.	.	x	x	.	.	.	.	.
Gospel of Truth	.	.	.	√	.	x	.	.	.	.	.	.	.	.	.	.
Gospel of the Twelve	.	.	.	.	.	.	.	.	.	x	.	.	.	.	.	.
Gospel of Peter	.	.	.	.	.	.	.	.	.	?	x	.	.	.	.	.
Gospel of Basilides	.	.	.	.	.	.	.	.	x	x	.	.	.	.	.	.
Gospel of the Egyptians	.	.	.	.	.	.	√	.	.	x	.	.	.	.	.	.
Gospel of the Hebrews	.	.	.	.	.	.	√	.	.	?	¿	.	.	.	.	.
Gospel of Matthias	.	.	.	.	.	.	.	.	.	x	x	.	.	.	.	.
Traditions of Matthias	.	.	.	.	.	.	√	.	.	.	.	.	.	.	.	.
Preaching of	.	.	.	√	.	.	√	.	.	v	.	.	.	.	.	.

	Ig	Po	M	Va	JM	Ir	C	T	MC	O	E	CS	A	D	P	V
Peter																
Acts of Andrew	.	.	.	.	.	.	.	.	x	.	.	.	.	.	.	.
Acts of Paul	.	.	.	.	.	.	.	x	.	?	¿	.	.	.	.	.
Acts of John	.	.	.	.	.	.	.	.	.	x	.	.	.	.	.	.
Epistle to the Laodiceans	.	.	.	.	.	.	.	.	?	.	.	.	.	.	.	◊
I Clement	.	.	.	.	.	√	√	.	.	?	.	.	.	√	.	.
Epistle of Barnabas	.	.	.	.	.	.	√	.	.	?	¿	√	.	√	.	.
Didache	.	.	.	.	.	.	√	.	.	?	¿	.	?	√	.	.
Shepherd of Hermas	.	.	.	.	.	√	√	?	?	?	¿	√	?	√	.	.
Apocalypse of Peter	.	.	.	.	.	.	√	.	√	.	¿	.	.	.	.	.

APPENDIX 3

Quotes of the Canon by Ignatius (37-108 A.D.) in His Letters to Various Persons and Churches

Ignatius quotes the Gospel according Matthew

Ignatius		Matthew
Eph. 14:2	No one who professes faith falls into sin, nor does one who has learned to love hate. "The tree is known by its fruit". Similarly, those who profess to be Christ's will be recognized by their actions. For what matters is not a momentary act of professing, but being persistently motivated by faith.	12:33
Smyr. 6:1	Let no one be misled: heavenly beings, the splendor of angels, and principalities, visible and invisible, if they fail to believe in Christ's blood, they too are doomed. "Let him accept it who can". Let no one's position swell in his head, for faith and love are everything -- there is nothing preferable to them.	19:12
Poly. 2:2	In all circumstances be "wise as a serpent", and perpetually "harmless as a dove". The reason you have a body as well as a soul is that you may win the favor of the visible world. But ask that you may have revelations of what is unseen. In that way you will lack nothing and have an abundance of every gift.	10:16

Appendices

Ignatius quotes I Thessalonians

Ignatius		I Thessalonians
Eph. 10:1	"Keep on praying" for others too, for there is a chance of their being converted and getting to God. Let them, then, learn from you at least from your actions.	5:17

Ignatius quotes Colossians

Ignatius		Colossians
Eph. 10:2	Return their bad temper with gentleness; their boasts with humility; their abuse with prayer. In the face of their error, be "steadfast in the faith". Return their violence with mildness and do not be intent on getting your own back.	1:23

Ignatius quotes I Corinthians

Ignatius		I Corinthians
Eph. 18:1	I am giving my life (not that it's worth much!) for the cross, which unbelievers find a stumbling block, but which means to us salvation and eternal life. "Where is the wise man? Where is the debater?" Where are the boasts of those supposedly intelligent?	1:20
Trall. 1:3	Those too who are deacons of Jesus	4:1

	Christ's "mysteries" must give complete satisfaction to everyone. For they do not serve mere food and drink, but minister to God's Church. They must therefore avoid leaving themselves open to criticism, as they would shun fire.	
Trall. 12:3	Out of love I want you to heed me, so that my letter will not tell against you. Moreover, pray for me. By God's mercy I need your love if I am going to deserve the fate I long for, and not prove a "castaway".	9:27
Rom. 5:1-2	Even now as a prisoner, I am learning to forgo my own wishes. All the way from Syria to Rome I am fighting with wild beasts, by land and sea, night and day, chained as I am to ten leopards (I mean to a detachment of soldiers), who only get worse the better you treat them. But by their injustices I am becoming a better disciple, "though not for that reason am I acquitted". What a thrill I shall have from the wild beasts that are ready for me! I hope they will make short work of me. I shall coax them on to eat me up at once and not to hold off, as sometimes happens, through fear.	4:4
Rom. 6:1	Not the wide bounds of earth nor the kingdoms of this world nor the kingdoms of this world will avail me anything. "I would rather die" and get to Jesus Christ, than reign over the ends of the earth. That is what I am looking for -- the One who died for us. That is whom I want -- the One who rose for us.	9:15

Ignatius quotes Romans

Ignatius		Romans
Eph. 20:2	I will do this especially if the Lord shows me that you are all, every one of you, meeting together under the influence of grace that we owe to the Name, in one faith and in union with Christ who was "descended from David according to the flesh" and is Son of man and Son of God. At these meetings you should heed the bishop and presbytery attentively, and break one loaf, which is the medicine of immortality, and the antidote which wards off death but yields continuous life in union with Jesus Christ.	1:3

Ignatius quotes Acts

Ignatius		Acts
Mag. 5:1	Yes, everything is coming to and end, and we stand before this choice -- death or life -- and everyone, will go "to his own place". Once might say similarly, there are two coinages, one God's, the other the world's. Each bears its own stamp -- unbelievers that of this world; believers, who are spurred by love, the stamp of God the Father through Jesus Christ. And if we do not willingly die in union with his Passion, we do not have his life in us.	1:25

Ignatius quotes Gospel according to Luke

Ignatius		Luke
Smyr. 3:1-2	For myself, I am convinced and believe that even after the resurrection he was in the flesh. Indeed, when he came to Peter and his friends,	24:39

he said to them, "Take hold of me, touch me and see that I am not a bodiless ghost.". And they at once touched him and were convinced, clutching his body and his very breath. For this reason they despised death itself, and proved its victors. Moreover, after the resurrection he ate and drank with them as a real human being, although in spirit he was united with the Father.

Ignatius quotes Ephesians

	Ephesians
God grant I may never forget it! By the grace which you have put on, I urge you to press forward in your race and to urge everybody to be saved. Vindicate your position by giving your whole attention to its material and spiritual sides. Make unity your concern -- there is nothing better than that. Lend everybody a hand, as the Lord does you. "Out of love be patient" with everyone, as indeed you are.	4:2
Tell my sisters to love the Lord and to be altogether contented with their husbands. Similarly urge my brothers in the name of Jesus Christ "to love their wives as the Lord loves the Church".[166]	5:25,29

---

[166] Quotes of Ignatius from the Canon in his letters. (www.ntcanon.org/Ignatius.shtml).

APPENDIX 4

Surviving a College Education

By Chuck Edwards
Summit Ministries
May 27, 2004

> "Our daughter was raised in Christian schools and in a Christian home where we taught her Christian values and morals...Two years out of high school at 20 [years] old, she enrolled at the University...Unfortunately she was overwhelmed by the professors and began to believe their philosophies. She graduated two years ago...and has turned her back on all that she believed in. We are trusting God to bring our girl back. The wait is sometimes difficult, but we are on bended knee."

How tragic! Yet this is just one example of a growing trend: kids reared in Christian homes that lose their faith at college. In fact, national surveys indicate that up to 51 percent of Christian students no longer claim to be "born again" by their senior year in college.[167]

---

[167] An article copied from a website, which is typical of information from other sources.
http://headlines.agapepress.org/archive/5/afa/272004ce.asp.

APPENDIX 5

RELEVANT QUOTES[168]

Luke 18:8b Nevertheless when the Son of man cometh, shall he find faith on the earth?

Dr. D. A. Waite said in 2003:

"May He keep the present and **future leaders** of our DBS faithful to our principles and God's Words without wavering." Message Book, 2003, p. 88]

Dr. Robert J. Barnett said in 2003:

"I told Dr. Waite I have a burden that **future generations** of the DBS will continue to hold the same firm stand on the inspiration of the Bible we hold today" [Message Book, 2003, p. 1]

Peter Lopez said in 2001:

"Being twenty-one years old and **a part of the younger generation,**...stout KJV Bible defenders are aging and even beginning to fade off the scene. [Can any forget David Otis Fuller, If the KJV is set aside, the truths presented and emphasized within it will be lost. Therefore, it is essential that the importance of a strong stand for the KJV be taught to those in **the next generation**....As I look around at **those in my generation I can't help but notice the lazy attitude towards defending God's Word (The King James Bible). Your children and grandchildren are in danger** of growing up without the truths of our Blessed King James Bible instilled within their hearts. The perpetuation of the KJV is scriptural, safe, and essential. **You must determine to teach those coming after you**

---

[168] Many of the following quotes were found at www.basicquotations.com/index.php?

that they may not be "A Truthless Generation." [DBS Message Book, 2001, pp. 37-40]

A young (20's) unmarried computer expert and member of this author's church said:

"My generation is out of control."

John Maynard Keynes said:

"Education: the inculcation of the incomprehensible into the indifferent by the incompetent."

Dr. Laurence J. Peter said:

Education is a method whereby one acquires a higher grade of prejudices.

Noah Webster said:

"Education is useless without the Bible." "In my view, the Christian religion is the most important and one of the first things in which all children, under a free government, ought to be instructed."

William Butler Yeats said:

"Education is not the filling of a pail, but the lighting of a fire."

Sir Winston Churchill said:

"Men occasionally stumble on the truth, but most of them pick themselves up and hurry off as if nothing had happened."

Adolf Hitler said:

"The victor will never be asked if he told the truth."

Arthur Wellesley said:

"Educate men without religion and you make of them but clever devils."

G. M. Trevelyan (1876-1962) British historian said:

"Education...has produced a vast population able to read but unable to distinguish what is worth reading."

Douglas Yates said:

"They say that we are better educated than our parents' generation. What they mean is that we go to school longer. They are not the same thing."

Oscar Wilde (1854-1900) said:

"Everyone who is incapable of learning has taken to teaching."

John Dewey said:

"I believe that education is the fundamental method of social progress and reform."

And:

"I believe that the community's duty to education is, therefore, its paramount moral duty. By law and punishment, by social agitation and discussion, society can regulate and form itself in a more or less haphazard and chance way. But through education society can formulate its own purposes, can organize its own means and resources, and thus shape itself with definiteness and economy in the direction in which it wishes to move. I believe that when society once recognizes the possibilities in this direction, and the obligations which these possibilities impose, it is impossible to conceive of the resources of time, attention, and money which will be put at the disposal of the educator. I believe that it is the business of every one interested in education to insist upon the school as the primary and most effective interest of social progress and reform in order that society may be awakened to realize what the school stands for, and aroused to the necessity of endowing the educator with sufficient equipment properly to perform his task. I believe that education thus conceived marks the most perfect and intimate union of science and art conceivable in human experience."

H. D. Williams said:

"The sodomites have demonstrated they understand that control of the beliefs of a society is through the educational system."

John Dewey said:

"We speak of education as shaping, forming, molding activity—that is, a shaping into the standard form of social activity."

Will Durante said:

"Education is the transmission of civilization."

John Dewey said:

"I believe that education is the fundamental method of social progress and reform. All reforms which rest simply upon the law, or the threatening of certain penalties, or upon changes in mechanical or outward arrangements, are transitory and futile.... But through education society can formulate its own purposes, can organize its own means and resources, and thus shape itself with definiteness and economy in the direction in which it wishes to move.... Education thus conceived marks the most perfect and intimate union of science and art conceivable in human experience. My Pedagogic Creed, 1897."

David Cloud said:

"Hundreds, even thousands, of salvations are claimed, though an extremely large percentage of these converts (up to even 99%) demonstrate no biblical evidence that the Spirit of God has regenerated them....When Mr. or Mrs. Average North America thinks of sin, he thinks of having a lack of self-esteem or of having a few relatively minor shortcomings, etc. He does not think of himself as having been born in sin (Ps. 51:5), and as having a heart that is deceitful above all things and desperately wicked (Jer. 17:9), and as having no true goodness or righteousness before God (Rom. 3:10,12; Is. 64:6); but this is precisely what the Bible says about each one of us." [HOW TO AVOID FALSE PROFESSIONS; Updated June 1, 2004 (first published September 27, 2002) (David Cloud, Fundamental Baptist Information Service, P.O. Box 610368, Port Huron, MI 48061, 866-295-4143, fbns@wayoflife.org;]

Dr. Harold Brown said:

"[N]o orthodox Christian will accept the implication of some thinkers, such as theologians Martin Werner of Berlin (1887-1964) and John A. T. Robinson of Cambridge (b.1919), that Christ was deceived or deceived his followers about the imminence of his return." [Brown, *Heresies,* p. 43]

And:

"During the early twentieth century, attempts were made to deny the historicity of Jesus." [Brown, Heresies, p. 45]

And:

"Many modern writers tried to claim that the Gospel of John was a late, Hellenistic, neo-platonic, postapostolic writing because of "logos" ideas, but the Dead Sea Scrolls have put that to bed. The logos idea has been a Semitic concept for a long time also." [Brown, p. 48, not quoted]

"The Pastor of Hermas was one of the most popular books, if not the most popular book, in the Christian Church during the second, third, and fourth centuries. It occupied a position analogous in some respects to that of Bunyan's *Pilgrim's Progress* in modern times; and critics have frequently compared the two works." [www.earlychristianwritings.com/info/shepherd.html]

[Easton's] "As to the time at which the Old Testament canon was closed, there are many considerations which point to that of Ezra and Nehemiah, immediately after the return from Babylonian exile."

APPENDIX 6

THE FORMATION OF THE NEW TESTAMENT CANON

[From *Forever Settled*, by Dr. Jack Moorman, p. 44-45]

After the New Testament books had been written, the next step in the divine program for the New Testament Scriptures was the gathering of these individual books into one New Testament canon in order that thus they might take their place beside the books of the Old Testament canon as the concluding portion of His Holy Word. Let us now consider how this was accomplished under the guidance of the Holy Spirit.

The first New Testament books to be assembled together were the Epistles of Paul. The Apostle Peter, shortly before he died, referred to Paul's Epistles as Scripture and in such a way as to indicate that at least the beginning of such a collection had already been made (II Peter 3:15-16). Even radical scholars, such as L. J. Goodspeed (1926), agree that a collection of Paul's Epistles was in circulation at the beginning of the second century and that Ignatius (117) referred to it. When the Four Gospels were collected together is unknown, but it is generally agreed that this must have taken place before 170 AD because at that time Tatian made his harmony of the Gospels (Diatessaron), which included all four of the canonical Gospels and only these four. Before 200 AD Paul, the Gospels, Acts, I Peter and I John were recognized as Scripture by Christians everywhere (as the writings of Irenaeus, Clement of Alexandria, and Tertullian prove) and accorded an authority equal to that of the Old Testament Scriptures. It was Tertullian, moreover, who first applied the name New Testament to this collection of apostolic writings.

The seven remaining books, 2 and 3 John, 2 Peter, Hebrews, James, Jude and Revelation, were not yet unanimously accepted as Scripture. By the time the fourth century had arrived, however, few Christians seem to have questioned the right of these disputed books to a place in the New Testament canon. Eminent Church Fathers of that era, such as Athanasius, Augustine, and Jerome, include them in their lists of the New Testament books. Thus through the Holy Spirit's guidance of individual believers, silently and gradually - but nevertheless surely, the Church as a whole was led to a recognition of the fact that the twenty-seven books of the New Testament, and only these books, form the canon which God gave to be placed beside the Old Testament Scriptures as the authoritative and final revelation of His will.

This guidance of the Holy Spirit was negative as well as positive. It involved not only the selection of canonical New Testament books but also the rejection of all non-canonical books which were mistakenly regarded as canonical by some of the early Christians. Thus the Shepherd of Hermas was used as holy Scripture by Irenaeus and Clement of Alexandria, and the same status was wrongly given to the Teaching of the Twelve Apostles by Clement and Origen. Clement likewise commented on the Apocalypse of Peter and the Epistle of Barnabas, to which Origen also accorded the title "catholic." And in addition, there were many false Gospels in circulation, as well as numerous false Acts ascribed to various Apostles. But although some of those non-canonical writings gained temporary acceptance in certain quarters, this state of affairs lasted for but a short time. Soon all Christians everywhere were led by the Holy Spirit to repudiate these spurious works and to receive only the canonical books as their New Testament Scriptures.

Having said all this, it must also be acknowledged that there is a deep and sacred mystery in the formation of the Written Word on Earth just as there had been in the incarnation and development of the Living Word (my comment, HDW).

APPENDIX 7

Crime Graphs[169]
Our Foundations Are being Destroyed

The incarceration rate has more than tripled since 1980.

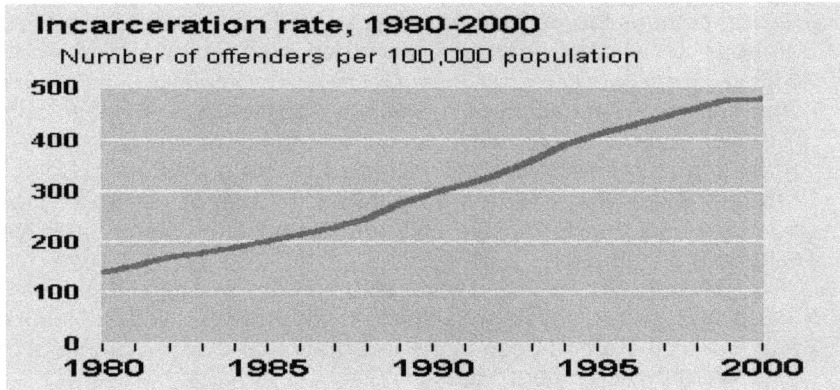

Source: Correctional Populations in the United States, 1997 and Prisoners in 2000.

Note: Number of sentenced inmates incarcerated under State and Federal jurisdiction per 100,000, 1980-00. BJS home page Social Statistics Briefing Room

---

[169] The following graphs were obtained from the US Department of Justice website, www.ojp.usdoj.gov/bjs/glance/tables/html in 2004. Shortly after copying them, they were removed from the site and different graphs were put up that seemed to favor law enforcement.

The number of arrests for drug abuse violations increased from 1999 to 2000 for both juveniles and adults.

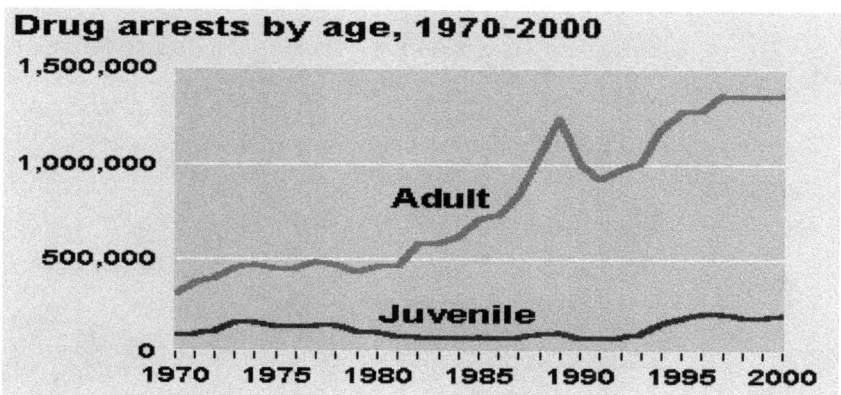

Source: FBI, The Uniform Crime Reports (UCR) Drug abuse violations are defined as State or local offenses relating to the unlawful possession, sale, use, growing, manufacturing, and making of narcotic drugs including opium or cocaine and their derivatives, marijuana, synthetic narcotics, and dangerous nonnarcotic drugs such as barbiturates. Juveniles are defined as persons under 18 years of age.

Adults are defined as persons 18 years old and older.

Over half of the increase in State prison population since 1990 is due to an increase in the prisoners convicted of violent offenses. To view data, click on the chart.

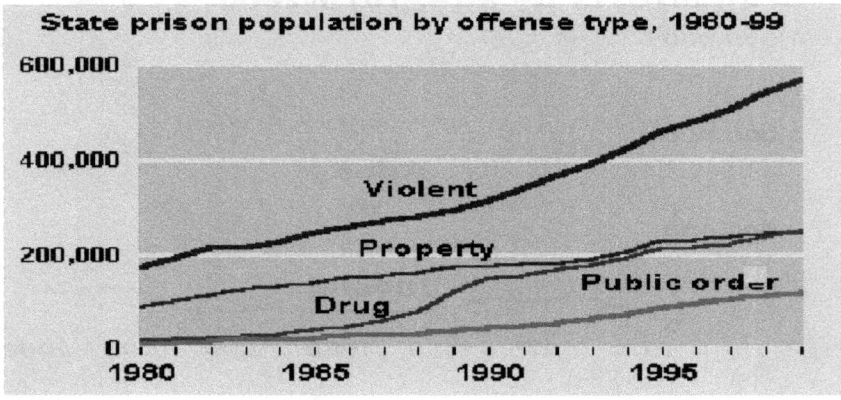

Source: Correctional Populations in the United States, 1997 and Prisoners in 2000. Violent offenses include murder, negligent and nonnegligent manslaughter, rape, sexual assault, robbery, assault, extortion, intimidation, criminal endangerment, and other violent offenses. Property offenses include burglary, larceny, motor vehicle theft, fraud, possession and selling of stolen property, destruction of property, trespassing, vandalism, criminal tampering, and other property offenses. Drug offenses include possession, manufacturing, trafficking, and other drug offenses. Public-order offenses include weapons, drunk driving, escape or flight to avoid prosecution, court offenses, obstruction, commercialized vice, morals and decency charges, liquor law violations, and other public-order offenses.

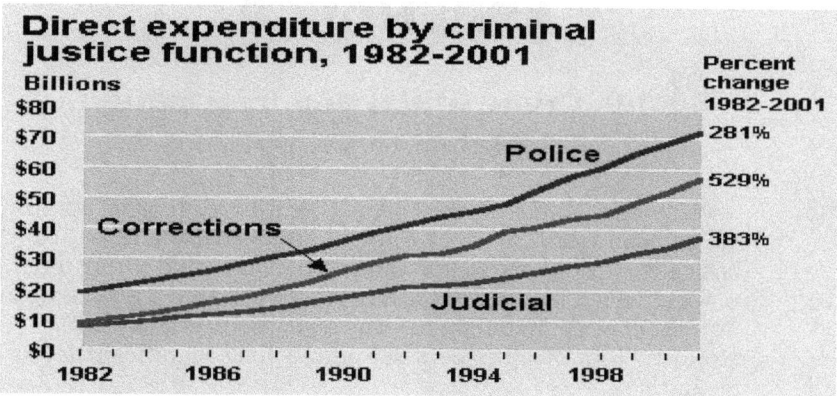

Cost of Crime is soaring.

APPENDIX 8

Social, Crime Stats, and Information Related to Crime.

1. Seventy-five % of students **admitted** to cheating on an exam. [Josephson Institute, 2002 Survey] Mr. Josephson says, "They're basically decent kids whose values are being totally corrupted by a world which is sanctioning stuff that even they know is wrong. But they can't understand why everybody allows it."[170] "It's typically 30% of all papers submitted have significant levels of plagiarism."[171]
2. "Intentional violence accounts for one-third of all injury deaths in the United States.
3. Intentional interpersonal violence disproportionately involves young people as both perpetrators and victims.
4. Among minority youth, particularly African Americans, violence has struck with unique force in recent years. Homicide has been the leading cause of death among African American males and females between the ages of 15-24 for more than ten years.
5. Firearm-related deaths among African American youth have particularly increased. Between 1984 and 1993, gun-related deaths of young African American males tripled, with the most dramatic rise among those 13 to 18 years old.
6. As levels of violence in the general society have risen sharply, it is a disturbing, but not surprising corollary that the levels of violence in and around schools have also increased.
7. Research suggests that violence in schools derives mainly from factors external to schools, but may be precipitated or aggravated by the school environment.
8. Student assaults on other students are the most frequent type of violence reported in schools.
9. In recent years, weapon carrying by students in schools has become a growing source of violence and threat of violence. A study by the Centers for Disease Control and Prevention (1995) found that nearly one-fourth of students nationwide had carried a weapon to school during the month preceding the survey.

---

[170] Gibson, Charles; *Caught Cheating*, Transcript of PrimeTime Live, 4/29/04.
[171] Ibid.

10. The personal health costs and economic costs to society from the devastation of violence are immense. Nationwide, the average cost of fatal and nonfatal violent injuries was $44,000 in 1992. The total medical cost of all violence that occurred in the United States was estimated at $13.5 billion in 1992."[172]
11. "Virtually all brokerages and market listed companies have passively or actively allowed fraudulent analyst reports and recommendations to boost their stock prices, or those of their clients, even though they falsely claimed that the analysts were independent. Apparently it was a well-known insiders game that ultimately caused enormous loss for all consumers who weren't in on the secret."[173]
12. Recent Department of Justice crime stats show a downturn in criminal activity. However, in order to receive federal funds a city or state must show improving stats. Our nearby city of Atlanta recently admitted to "underreporting" crime stats by a huge percent because of the desire to obtain government funds. Most reliable stats show a continued worsening of crime or a significant increase in expenditures related to "control" of crime.
13. "This is not an isolated problem (the Columbine Massacre and "Trench Coat Mafia). Following the massacre, schools around the country have received scores of threats from other weird-minded young people who promise to exercise more violence. Several students have been arrested prior to committing similar atrocities and the police have confiscated the weapons they were planning to use."[174]

---

[172] Center For The Study and Prevention of Violence, School Violence Fact Sheets www.colorado.edu/cspv/publications/factsheets/schoolviolence/FS-SV02.html.
[173] *Corporate Fraud*; http://crime.org/links_academic.html.
[174] Way of Life, *How To Keep Kids Out Of The Trench Coat Mafia*, David Cloud, 6/03/04 email from Fundamental Baptist Information Service.

APPENDIX 9

Approximate Number of Speculative Terms Occurring in Bart Ehrman's *Lost Christianities*,

SPECULATIVE TERM	OCCURRENCES OVER 257 PAGES
1. "If"	118
2. "Probably"	37
3. "Appears"	38
4. "Appear"	18
5. "Maybe" or "May be"	26
6. "Perhaps"	2
7. "Could be"	5
8. "Although he obviously doesn't say so"	1
9. "May have"	13
10. "Nearly made"	2
11. "Is it because"	3
12. Could they have been?"	1
13. "We can never know for certain"	2
14. "Possibly"	52
15. "Suspicion"	1
16. "Suggesting that"	1
17. "Might be"	2
18. "Suppose"	4
19. "Presumably"	9
20. "We do not know"	6
21. "Predictably"	2
22. "Evidently"	25
TOTAL	417—or 1.62 occurrences/PAGE

This amounts to 7 times more speculative terms/Page than occurs in Dean John William Burgon's work! See the next chart.

APPROXIMATE SPECULATIVE TERMS OCCURRING IN DEAN BURGON'S *REVISION REVISED*

SPECULATIVE TERM	OCCURRENCES OVER 25 PAGES
"If"	2
"Probably"	1
"It is thought"	2
"Suppose"	1
TOTAL	6—or 0.24 Occurrences/PAGE

APPENDIX 10

Exercise Care Reading the Following Books:

a. *Lost Christianities* (by Bart D. Ehrman)
b. *The Canon Debate* (Lee McDonald, James A. Sanders)
c. *The New Testament, Historical Introduction To The Early Christian Writings* (Bart D. Ehrman)
d. *Evolution, Science, and Scripture* (Warfield)
e. *The Bible In Translation Ancient and English Versions* (Bruce Metzger)
f. *The Text Of The New Testament Its Transmission, Corruption, and Restoration* (Bruce Metzger)
g. *Lost Scriptures, Books That Did Not Make It Into The New Testament* (Bart D. Ehrman)
h. *The Canon Of Scripture* (F. F. Bruce)
i. *The Canon Of The New Testament* (Bruce Metzger)
j. *The New Testament: Its Background, Growth, and Content* (Bruce Metzger)
k. *Introduction To Biblical Interpretation* (Klien, Blomberg, Hubbard)

BIBLIOGRAPHY

Barnett, Dr. Robert J. "The King James Bible Authority." *The Dean Burgon Society Messages.* From the 22nd Annual Meeting, #10. Collingswood, NJ. Bible For Today #2999-P.
_____ "Turretin." *DBS Message Book.* Collingwood, NJ. 1991.
Brown, Ph.D., Harold O. J. *Heresies.* Peabody, Massachusetts. Hendrickson Publishers. 1988.
Bruce, F. F. *The Canon of Scripture.* Downer's Grove, IL. Intervarsity Press. 1988.
Burgon, Dean John William. *The Revision Revised.* Collingswood, NJ. The Dean Burgon Society Press. Originally published 1880's, republished 2000.
Cloud, David W. *Way of Life Encyclopedia of the Bible and Christianity, 4th Edition.* Port Huron, MI. Way of Life Literature. 2002.
_____ "Biblical Inspiration, Part I." Port Huron, MI. Way of Life Literature. June 14, 2004.
Dean Burgon Society News. Collingswood, NJ. Dean Burgon Society Press.
Easton, *Easton's 1897 Bible Dictionary.* Austin TX. Wordsearch iExalt Electronic Publishing, Ver. 5.
Ehrman, Bart D. *Lost Christianities, The Battle For Scripture and the Faiths We Never Knew.* New York, NY. Oxford University Press. 2003.
_____ *Misquoting Jesus, The Story Behind Who Changed the Bible and Why.* Harper Collins Publishers. San Francisco, CA. 2005.
_____ *Truth and Fiction in The Da Vinci Code.* New York, NY. Oxford University Press. 2004.
_____ *Lost Scriptures, Books that Did Not Make It into the New Testament.* New York, NY. Oxford University Press. 2003
Erickson, Millard J. Erickson. *The Postmodern World.* Wheaton, IL. Crossway Books. 2002.
Green, Jay P. *Unholy Hands on the Bible;* Vol. II. Lafayette, IN. Sovereign Grace Trust Fund. 1992.
Jones, Dr. Floyd Nolan Jones. *The Chronology of the Old Testament.* Green Forrest, AR. Master Books. 2005.
Jackson, Wayne. "The Remarkable Robert Dick Wilson" *Christian Courier.* April 2000. www.christiancourier.com/penpoints/rdWilson.htm
Irenaeus, *Against Heresies.* http://www.ccel.org/fathers/ANF-01/iren/iren4.html#Section20. Accessed March, 2004.

Klein, Dr. W. W., Dr. Craig L. Blomberg, Dr. R. L. Hubbard, Jr. *Introduction To Biblical Interpretation*. Nashville, TN. 1993.

LaMore, Dr. Gary L. *"Wilbur Pickering's Surprise Ending" Dean Burgon Society Message Book*. Collingswood, NJ. Dean Burgon Society Press. 2003.

McDonald, Lee M., and James A. Sanders, Editors. *The Canon Debate*. Peabody, MA. Hendrickson Publishers. 2002.

Metzger, Bruce M. *The New Testament, Its Background, Growth, and Content*, 3rd Edition. Nashville, TN. Abingdon Press. 2003.

Moorman, Dr. Jack. *Early Church Fathers and the Authorized Version, A Demonstration*. Collingswood, NJ. Bible For Today Press. This has been released in hardback as: Early Manuscripts, Church Fathers, and the Authorized Version. 2005.

_____*Forever Settled*. Collingswood, NJ. Dean Burgon Society Press.

Pickering, Wilbur, *The Identity of the New Testament Text*. Nashville, TN. Thomas Nelson Publishers. 1980.

Sanders, James A. "The Family in the Bible." *Biblical Theology Bulletin*. Seton Hall University. South Orange, NJ. Fall, 2002.

Strouse, Dr. Thomas. "The Translation Model Predicted by Scripture." Newington, CN. Emmanuel Baptist Theological Seminary. www.emmanuel-newington.org/seminary/resources/KJV_Model.pdf.

_____ *The Lord Hath Spoken: A Guide To Bibliology*. Newington, CT. Emmanuel Baptist Theological Press. 1998.

_____ "Scholarly Myths Perpetuated on Rejecting the Masoretic Text of the OT." *Dean Burgon Society Message Book*. Collingswood, NJ. Dean Burgon society Press. 2003.

Sightler, M.D., Dr. James H. *A Testimony Founded For Ever*. Greenville, SC. Sightler Publications. 2nd Edition, 2001.

Thieleman, J. van Braght. *Martyrs Mirror*. Scottdale, PA. Herald Press. 1950.

Theiss, George. "Which Bible?" www.tulipgems.com/WhichBible2.htm.

Waite, Th.D., Ph.D., Dr. D. A. "How We Got Our Bible," http://www.deanburgonsociety.org/howbible.htm

_____ *Defending the King James Bible*. Collingswood, NJ. Bible For Today Press. 1995.

_____ *The Case For The KJV*. Collingswood, NJ. Bible For Today Press. BFT # 83.

_____ *The Heresies of Westcott and Hort*. Collingswood, NJ. Bible For Today Press.

Williams, M.D., Ph.D., H. D. *The Pure Words of God, Where to Find*

God's Words Which We Are Commanded to Receive and Keep. Cleveland, GA. The Old Paths Publications. 2008.

_____ *The Septuagint is a Paraphrase, The Character of God's Words is Not Found in the LXX or the "G."* Cleveland, GA. The Old Paths Publications. 2008.

_____ *The Lie That Changed The Modern World, A Refutation of the Modernist Cry: "Poly-Scripturae."* Collingswood, NJ. Bible For Today Press. 2004.

_____ *Hearing the Voice of God.* Cleveland, GA. The Old Paths Publications. 2008.

Websites of Interest

www.theoldpathspublications.com
www.biblefortoday.org
www.deanburgonsociety.org
www.svchapel.org/Assets/Docs/DoctrinalStatement.pdf
http://mb-soft.com/believe/txc/tubingen.htm
www.didjesusexist.com/marcion.html.
www.ntcanon.org/Peshitta.shtml
www.ntcanon.org/table.shtml
www.fact-index.com/f/fe/fenton_john_anthony_hort.html
www.christiancourier.com
www.basicquotations.com
www.ojp.usdoj.gov

INDEX

Abbreviations, 5, 9
adaptability, 45
Adoptionists, 71
Adversus Haereses, 105, 106
AFTs, 9, 34
Against Heresies, 97, 105, 106, 161
Aland (Kurt), 32, 68, 102, 111
Albigensians, 83
Aleph, 43
Alexandria, 11, 12, 66, 84, 96, 135
Alexandrian, 11, 12, 30, 41, 42, 43, 67
Alexandrians, 41
Alexandrinus, 43
anachronism, 15, 26
Ancient of Days, 117
Antiochian, 32
Apocalypse of Peter, 103, 137, 151
apocrypha, 11, 12, 23, 66, 134
apograph, 11, 41, 59
Apostles, 11, 12, 15, 20, 21, 24, 25, 39, 63, 81, 98, 118, 133, 151
argumentum ad hominem, 48, 83
Arian(ism), 66, 80, 81
Asceticism, 89
Athanasius, 83, 84, 135, 150
attraction(s), 88, 89
B manuscript, 43
Babylonian, 83, 86, 94, 132, 149
Baptist, 11, 13, 23, 27, 148, 157, 162, 171
Barna, 122
Barnes (Albert), 81
Barnett (Robert), 34, 35, 40, 73, 144, 161

Barth (Karl), 29
Baruch, 31, 58, 59
Basilides, 95, 136
Bauer (Walter), 90, 92
Baur (F. C.), 29, 90, 91, 92
Beza MS, 43
Brandenburg (Kent), 46
Brown (Harold O. J.), 75, 80, 85, 86, 87, 88, 90, 95, 96, 100, 124, 148, 149, 161
Bruce (F. F.), 58, 68, 84, 96, 97, 100, 102, 107, 159, 161, 162
Burgon (Dean John William), 40, 48, 67, 158, 161, 162, 171
Canon criticism, 31
Canon Debate, 26, 27, 28, 37, 43, 45, 46, 51, 63, 65, 69, 85, 87, 93, 101, 102, 111, 112, 159, 162
Canon of Scripture, 9, 11, 12, 17, 33, 37, 40, 43, 46, 48, 52, 55, 64, 69, 72, 74, 76, 84, 89, 93, 96, 97, 98, 100, 107, 111, 127, 161
Canon Seminar, 69
canon within a canon, 101
canonical, 30, 33, 34, 36, 37, 38, 39, 40, 41, 45, 46, 69, 72, 73, 86, 97, 98, 99, 101, 102, 103, 107, 109, 112, 127, 150, 151
Carpocratians, 71
Charismatic, 12, 89
Chenoboskion, 79
children, 5, 6, 47, 102, 122, 124, 125, 126, 128
Christianities, 74, 75, 82, 102
Clement of Alexandria, 103, 134, 150, 151
Codex, 12

Colwell (E. C.), 38
common-language translations, 67
Copies, 6, 58
Cosmos, 94
Council of Trent, 23, 102
creation(ism), 22, 24, 86, 88, 90, 93, 94
Crime Graphs, 7, 152
Crime Stats, 7, 156
critical text (CT), 9, 12, 27, 31, 37, 38, 40, 41, 43, 72, 162
Curse, 7, 121
D (manuscript), 43
Dead Sea Scrolls (DSS), 9, 28, 63, 149
Dean Burgon Society (DBS), 9, 31, 34, 37, 40, 47, 48, 57, 61, 62, 67, 73, 116, 144, 145, 161, 162, 171
debate, 5, 18, 66
deconstructionism, 30
deductive (logic), 22, 23
Definitions, 5, 11
Denial, 86
Department of Justice, 122, 152, 157
dialectical materialism, 12, 90
Dialogue with Trypho, 39
dispensation, 46
Docetism, 87
Docetists, 71
Dualism, 87
Ebionites, 71
ekklesia, 46
Elihu, 49, 50, 51, 52
Emerson (Ralph Waldo), 15
emperors, 57
Engels, 90
ERV, 9, 67
Essenes, 27, 64
Eusebius, 134, 135
evolution, 88, 86, 95, 159
ex nihilo, 25

feminism, 30
Fuller (David Otis), 47, 144
Game, 6, 105
genealogical, 72, 115
Gnosticism, 5, 6, 12, 20, 21, 70, 75, 77, 80, 87, 88, 93, 94, 95
Gnostics, 1, 5, 6, 20, 51, 65, 70, 77, 79, 80, 81, 85, 87, 88, 89, 92, 94, 95, 98, 105
Green (Jay P.), 37, 79, 97, 161
Griesbach, 67
Haggadah, 29
Halakah, 29
Hebrew Masoretic Text, 23
Hegelian, 92
Hellenistic, 80, 86, 96, 149
Helvidius, 67
hermeneutics, 30
Hobbes, 29
Hort, 9, 32, 38, 48, 67, 72, 109, 115, 162
humanistic, 14, 24, 30, 90, 92, 93, 95, 112
Ignatius, 7, 99, 134, 138, 142, 150
inductive (hermeneutics), 22
inference, 86
Inscripturated Words, 12
inserts, 7, 107
inspiration, 5, 13, 50, 71, 161
intellectuals, 18
inventions, 126, 128
Irenaeus, 97, 103, 105, 106, 107, 134, 150, 151, 161
Jamnia (Council of), 26, 28, 87
Jeremiah, 31, 58, 59, 118, 125
Jerome, 23, 67, 102, 150
Josiah, 60, 61
jots and tittles, 22, 32, 33, 54, 69, 117
Jovinian, 67
Judaism, 20, 93, 96
Justin Martyr, 39, 100, 134
kanon, 33, 35, 38

Index

kerygma, 30
Ketubim, 9, 15, 26
King Jehoiakim, 31, 58, 97
Lachmann, 67
Latin Vulgate, 11, 15, 23, 67, 102
liberation theology, 30
Logos, 93
Lollards, 83
Lost Christianities, 7, 45, 58, 64, 70, 72, 73, 82, 84, 85, 86, 89, 90, 91, 92, 96, 98, 100, 103, 107, 108, 112, 127, 158, 159, 161
Lucian (recension), 32, 109
LXX, 6, 9, 11, 65, 66, 163
lying words, 66
Marcion, 6, 79, 81, 95, 96, 97, 98, 134
Marcionites, 71, 98
Marcosians, 71
Mariolatry, 15, 28, 94
Marx (Karl), 90
McDonald (Lee Martin), 26, 29, 45, 63, 65, 69, 87, 101, 112, 159, 162
measure, 11, 33, 34, 35, 36
Metzger (Bruce), 58, 68, 79, 87, 100, 102, 111, 159, 162
modern, 1, 5, 6, 21, 32, 67, 72, 83, 94, 122, 163, 171
Montanists, 71
Montanus, 85
Moorman (Jack), 31, 41, 42, 150, 162
Mormon, 79
Muratorium Canon, 98
Mystery, 5, 24
Mysticism, 13
Nag Hammadi, 64, 79, 83, 84, 102
NASB, 67
naturalistic textual critics, 43
Nebiim, 9, 15, 26, 62

Neo-Evangelicalism, 13
Neo-Orthodoxy, 14
NIV, 9, 67
NLB, 9, 67
Northern Italy, 67
Origen, 11, 65, 66, 81, 96, 135, 151
ostrich, 5, 52
parousia, 14, 65
Pesher, 29
Peshitta, 100, 109, 135, 163
Philo, 96
Pickering (Wilbur N.), 37, 38, 39, 40, 99, 109, 162
Platonism, 93
plenary, 14, 74, 107, 125, 127, 171
Polycarp, 134
postmodern(ism), 5, 13, 14, 21, 161
Protestant(s), 11, 23, 102
proto-Christians, 23, 70
proto-documents, 115
proto-orthodox, 14, 23, 30, 70, 71, 72, 73, 75, 82, 91, 127
pseudonymous, 32, 72, 86, 107
Q document, 109
Q source, 87, 97
qaneh, 33
Quelle, 109
Qumran, 27, 29, 63
Rabbinic Judaism, 29
Received Text (RT), 9, 11, 13, 14, 15, 23, 31, 40, 42, 59, 171
recension, 109
redaction criticism, 30, 109
Reformation, 15, 30
relevance, 45
revisionists, 72
rule, 11, 29, 33, 34, 35, 36, 101, 128
Ryle (H. C.), 28
Sacred Wisdom, 19
Sagan (Carl), 94

Samaritans, 27, 64
Sanders (James A.), 26, 29, 51, 52, 63, 69, 86, 87, 89, 159, 162
Satan, 23, 118
Saturnilus, 95
Saturninus, 95
scarlet thread, 24, 50
scholarolatry, 5, 15, 28, 32, 45, 46, 47
scholasticism, 20, 30, 75, 80, 94, 96
Scientific Investigation of the Old Testament, 132
seed of apostasy, 31
Semler, 67
Septuagint, 6, 9, 11, 65, 66, 163, 171
Shepherd of Hermas, 37, 84, 103, 105, 106, 107, 137, 151
Sinaiticus, 43, 135
Sinope, 95
speculative (terms), 7, 158
Spinoza, 29
spoof, 106
standard, 11, 34, 36, 40, 147
Strouse (Thomas), 13, 27, 33, 37, 39, 62, 84, 162
structuralism, 30
Subordinists, 71
Supposition, 86
synod of Jamnia, 26
TaNaK, 9, 15, 26, 27
Tatian, 100, 150
Tendencies, 6, 88
Theodotians, 71
Thomas, 13, 27, 29, 33, 37, 38, 62, 109, 136, 162
threw, 46, 53
toleration, 13
Torah, 9, 15, 26, 65
Traditional Text (TT), 9, 11, 15, 23, 31, 32, 40, 42, 59, 109
Transcendentalism, 15

Tubingen, 90, 91, 92
Turretin, 34, 35, 73, 161
U.S. News, 69
Unitarian, 79
Valentinians, 71
Vaticanus, 43
Vulgate, 135
W/H, 9
Waite (Dr. D. A.), 47, 57, 59, 62, 63, 67, 144, 162
Waldensians, 67, 83
Way of Life Encyclopedia, 36, 39, 109, 161
Westcott, 9, 32, 48, 67, 72, 162
Wiccan, 79
Williams (Dr. H. D.), 1, 2, 3, 19, 29, 32, 52, 66, 67, 72, 83, 89, 99, 129, 147, 162, 171
Wilson (Robert Dick), 7, 63, 131, 133, 161
Wisdom of Solomon, 103
Yavneh, 26

ABOUT THE AUTHOR

Dr. Williams was born in Ft. Pierce, Florida. He was saved at the age of fourteen at his local Baptist church where he was active in the church youth group. His local church ordained him to preach the gospel. After graduating with honors from high school, he attended Stetson University where he met his wife, Patricia, and they were married in 1961. Starting in the ministerial program at Stetson and switching to pre-med in his junior year, he graduated with honors with a B.A. After Stetson, he taught high school at Eau Gallie, Florida for two years, and then continued his training at the University of Miami Medical School where he graduated with honors. Following his medical training, Dr. Williams and Patricia settled in New Port Richey, Florida where he practiced Family Medicine as a board certified family practitioner. He was active in his community as a hospital board member for twenty years, a chief-of-staff, president of the medical society, an advisory board member and president of Moody Bible Institute's Florida program, a board member of the Health Planning Commission, and a teacher at his local Baptist church. He helped develop and administrate a multi-specialist medical clinic with forty thousand patients and seventeen doctors. His Biblical training was obtained at Stetson University, Moody Bible Institute, and Louisiana Baptist University. After retirement, Dr. Williams has continued serving the Lord Jesus Christ as an associate pastor, a teacher, and as vice-president and representative for the Dean Burgon Society. He received a Ph.D. in Biblical studies at Louisiana Baptist University. He has traveled to many foreign lands where he has represented the Dean Burgon Society, teaching pastors and participating in evangelistic events. He is author of several books; *The Lie That Changed The Modern World; Word-For-Word Translating of the Received Texts, Verbal Plenary Translating; Hearing the Voice of God; The Septuagint is a Paraphrase;* and *The Pure Words of God,* in addition to many articles and booklets. Dr. Williams and his wife, Patricia have two sons and five grandchildren.

OTHER BOOKS BY DR. WILLIAMS

HEARING THE VOICE OF GOD:
    This 264 page perfect bound book will be released in January, 2008. ISBN 978-0-9801689-0-7. You will be able to purchase it at Amazon.com. or at BibleForToday.org, BFT # **3340**.
    Dr. Williams' book, *Hearing the Voice of God*, discusses the critical factors related to the postmodern confusion surrounding this issue. He approaches the subject clearly and realistically from a biblicist's point of view. Mysticism is refuted. Individuals desiring the truth about God speaking to them will appreciate this volume. Many present day teachers encourage emotionally distressed people to turn to their own thoughts, as if their thoughts were God speaking to them. This work investigates the topic as it relates to revelation, conscience, inspiration, illumination, and the voice of the Lord in Scripture. Dr. Williams explains how postmodern philosophy has created an atmosphere that contributes to the confusion surrounding this important subject. www.theoldpathspublications.com, or www.biblefortoday.org.

WORD-FOR-WORD TRANSLATING OF THE RECEIVED TEXTS, VERBAL PLENARY TRANSLATING:
    This 264 page perfect bound book may be purchased through www.BibleForToday.org. See below. There is a vital need for a book to inform sincere Bible-believing Christians about the proper techniques of translating the WORDS of God into the receptor languages of the world. No book like this one has ever been written. It is a unique and much-needed book. The very first requirement for any translation of the Bible is to have the proper WORDS of Hebrew, Aramaic, and Greek from which to translate. It is the contention of this book that the original verbally and plenarily inspired Hebrew, Aramaic, and Greek WORDS have been verbally and plenarily preserved in accordance with God's promises. These preserved WORDS are those received-text-WORDS which underlie the King James Bible. This volume emphasizes the requirement of a proper technique to be used in all translations of God's WORDS. It must be done in a verbally and plenarily translation technique. That is, the Hebrew, Aramaic, and Greek WORDS must be conveyed into the receptor languages, not merely the ideas, concepts, thoughts, or message. This technique is absent in all of the other manuals on Bible translation. Dr. Williams is not the usual sort of writer. He combines the meticulous skill of a Doctor of Medicine with the artistry and acumen of a Doctor of Philosophy to produce this grand volume. May translators and sincere Christians of all

persuasions and professions use this important book worldwide! The Bible For Today Press, BFT #**3302**
ISBN 1-56848-056-3, Order by PHONE: 1-800-JOHN 10:9, Order by FAX: 856-854-2464, Order by MAIL: Bible For Today, 900 Park Avenue, Collingswood, NJ 08108"

THE ATTACK ON THE CANON OF SCRIPTURE, A POLEMIC AGAINST MODERN SCHOLARSHIP

This 264 page perfect bound book will be released in January, 2008. ISBN 978-0-9801689-0-7. This 152 page book demonstrates the newest attack on the Words and books of the Bible by modern day scholarship. The changing methods for assaulting the Scriptures are important for those who are concerned about the relentless attempt to destroy them. In a remarkable polemic against modern scholarship, Dr. Williams outlines the most recent means many are using to undermine confidence in the Words of God received through the priesthood of believers. It will be available at Amazon.com. or at BibleForToday.org, BFT # **3340**.

THE LIE THAT CHANGED THE MODERN WORLD

This book is in hardback format, 440 pages in all. ISBN 1-56848-042-3. It is a factual defense not only of the King James Bible, but also of the Hebrew and Greek Words that underlie the King James Bible. The author is a medical doctor, now retired, who has researched this important topic thoroughly. May the Lord Jesus Christ use and honor this study in the days, weeks, months, and years ahead until our Lord Jesus Christ returns. It should be in every layman's library, every Pastor's library, every church library, every college library, every university library, and in every theological seminary library. It is available through Bible For Today Press, www.biblefortoday.org, BFT # **3125**.

THE PURE WORDS OF GOD

This is a perfect bound 136 page book. ISBN 978-0-9801689-1-4. Dr. Williams' book, *The Pure Words of God,* clarifies the use of the word "pure" when it is used to define the Words of God. Should "pure" be applied to translations, to Traditional/Received Texts, or to critical texts? Once the correct application is explained, Dr. Williams clarifies God's commands to receive and keep His pure Words. It is available through Amazon.com or Bible For Today Press at www.biblefortoday.org, BFT #**3344**.

www.ingramcontent.com/pod-product-compliance
Lightning Source LLC
Chambersburg PA
CBHW051836090426
42736CB00011B/1827